"In this prudent exploration
ences, Ron Cole-Turner cons.
medicines but also the risks to the church of discounting spiritual
experiences associated with psychedelics. An exceptional theological ethicist, Cole-Turner also writes as a pastor—someone
dedicated to the care of souls—asking: Is there room in the church
(or in science) for people who have psychedelic experiences that
defy clear rational explanation?"

—TRACY J. TROTHEN,
co-author of *Religion and the Technological Future: An
Introduction to Biohacking, AI, and Transhumanism*

"In this tour de force, Ron Cole-Turner takes us on a journey
exploring the intersection between psychedelics and Christianity.
In the next decade as the impact of psychedelics on the mental
health sector continues, the all-important question of mystical
and spiritual experiences needs urgent attention. There is no
better book available than the one on offer here to help with this.
It is groundbreaking in its historical, theological, cultural, and
scientific perspectives. With both thoroughness and clarity, it will
become a marker for all further conversations to come."

—BRIAN MACALLAN,
University of Divinity, Pilgrim Theological College

"If we have the opportunity to show up in an informed and engaged
manner, it is thanks to Cole-Turner preparing and equipping us to
do so. This will be required reading for any Christian interested
in a serious, accessible, balanced treatment of this most pressing
cultural, medical, and spiritual development. It will be used in
training psychedelic chaplains and in seminary courses devoted to
the church in its social context as well as pastoral care and spiritual
formation programs. Unequivocally, we are in Cole-Turner's debt
for this volume."

—JAIME CLARK-SOLES,
professor of New Testament, Perkins School of Theology,
Southern Methodist University

"The 'psychedelic renaissance' has commenced, with linkages between psychedelics, mental health, and spiritual experience evident. Theologian and ethicist Ron Cole-Turner ably guides through challenges such as nature of the linkages, societal and ecclesial acceptance, integration of the experience, and safety. Decades—or perhaps just years—from now, psychedelics hopefully will be normalized in mental health and spirituality. This book will register as key in that transition, with faith leaders and religion scholars benefitting."

—CALVIN MERCER,
professor of religion, East Carolina University

Psychedelics and Christian Faith

Psychedelics *and* Christian Faith

*Exploring an Unexpected Pathway
to Healing and Spirituality*

RON COLE-TURNER

Foreword by Hunt Priest

 CASCADE *Books* • Eugene, Oregon

PSYCHEDELICS AND CHRISTIAN FAITH
Exploring an Unexpected Pathway to Healing and Spirituality

Cascade Books
An Imprint of Wipf and Stock Publishers
199 W. 8th Ave., Suite 3
Eugene, OR 97401

www.wipfandstock.com

PAPERBACK ISBN: 978-1-6667-7899-1
HARDCOVER ISBN: 978-1-6667-7900-4
EBOOK ISBN: 978-1-6667-7901-1

Cataloguing-in-Publication data:

Names: Cole-Turner, Ronald, 1948–, author. | Priest, Hunt, foreword.

Title: Psychedelics and christian faith : exploring an unexpected pathway to
healing and spirituality / Ron Cole-Turner ; foreword by Hunt Priest.

Description: Eugene, OR : Cascade Books, 2025 | Includes bibliographical refer-
ences and index.

Identifiers: ISBN 978-1-6667-7899-1 (paperback) | ISBN 978-1-6667-7900-4
(hardcover) | ISBN 978-1-6667-7901-1 (ebook)

Subjects: LCSH: Alternative medicine—Religious aspects—Christianity. | Alter-
native medicine—Moral and ethical aspects—Christianity. | Hallucinogenic
drugs—Therapeutic use. | Hallucinogenic drugs—Spirituality. | Hallucino-
genic drugs—Public opinion. | Mental illness—Alternative treatment.

Classification: R733 .C64 2024 (paperback) | R733 .C64 (ebook)

VERSION NUMBER 01/21/25

Contents

Foreword

I am an Episcopalian and a priest. As an adult, I learned to keep ecstatic spiritual experiences at a safe and respectful distance. Thankfully though, on two separate occasions, a month apart, in February and March of 2016, I had two highly charged and life-changing encounters with the Holy Spirit. My vocation, my ministry, my personal and professional life would never be the same.

These two encounters were not in a church building, on a mountaintop, nor anywhere near fierce desert wilderness, although experiences of God in such places were not foreign to me. In the late winter of 2016, in the middle of my mid-life, I twice found myself lying on a sofa in a treatment room turned cozy den at the Johns Hopkins Bayview Medical Center in Baltimore. I was wearing eye shades, headphones offering music from a curated playlist, and had just ingested the prescribed "medium-high" doses of psilocybin, the active ingredient in "magic mushrooms." Well prepared and well cared for, I would be guided by members of the world's leading psychedelic research team.

I was on that sofa in Baltimore because I saw an ad and an article in *The Christian Century*, inviting religious professionals who had never used psychedelics to apply to be a participant in the groundbreaking mental health research that Dr. Roland Griffiths and the team at Hopkins had been doing since 2000. They had picked up where the destructive and politically motivated War on Drugs had stopped the psychedelic research in its tracks in the early 1970s.

What the researchers were discovering was that the people having the best results with treatment for their depression, anxiety, addiction, trauma, and fear of dying were also having profound religious and spiritual experiences. How might leaders from the world's religious traditions respond to the same protocols? To be included in this endeavor was a gift of a lifetime.

At fifty-one years old, a lifelong Christian and ordained leader in the Episcopal Church, I had discerned my call to the priesthood almost twenty years before at the Church of the Holy Comforter in Atlanta. Unlike any church I had ever known, 80 percent of the congregation lived with severe and persistent mental illness and resided in group care homes. The remaining 20 percent drove the vans, paid the bills, facilitated the twice-weekly arts programs, and helped tend the organic garden. The 80 percent were not a do-good project of the 20 percent. Together, we were the congregation; we were the church.

I saw, joined, and was forever changed by the church being the church, being in community Sunday after Sunday, Wednesday night after Wednesday night, with those so often rejected by the wider culture. It was the first but not the last time I was brought to tears by one of the promises Episcopalians say at our baptism, "With God's help, I will strive for justice and peace among all people, and respect the dignity of every human being."

Following seminary and ordination, multiple moves, and in the midst of this second career and what I believe is my vocation, I had created some distance with the Spirit that was seeming a bit too irrational and certainly uncontrollable. I had a church to run, after all. And while I did not doubt that I and others, whether in scripture or in modern life, had experienced profound movements of the Spirit, I had by 2016 taken a more rational approach to all of it, thank you very much.

I have shared some of my spiritual and religious experiences with psychedelics elsewhere, but among the primary religious and/or mystical experiences occasioned by those first two experiences with psilocybin: I spoke in tongues, sensed the Holy Spirit moving through my body as a powerful energetic force, experienced and was relieved of an extreme blockage of my throat chakra (a spiritual concept I was only vaguely aware of then), and had my ordination to the priesthood completed "at the feet of the Universe."

In a vision that seemed all too real, I was driving my family and close friends in a motorboat on a picture-perfect, seemingly endless day. The light was glistening off the water, all of us laughing with heads tossed back, we were looping around the large lake in perfect figure-8s (the infinity symbol). At some point, we had to refuel. I confidently sidled up to the dock (I'm not a boater) and a crew of smiling and energetic dockhands, women and men, filled the gas tank, tossed supplies into the boat, and told us to have a wonderful time. I believe that in that vision, the Spirit, God, Jesus, my own psyche, some combination of it all, were reminding me that all has been, is, and will be well, I have everything I need, and there are lots of people who want to help.

Fast forward nearly five years. I knew my experiences at Hopkins had forever changed my ministry, but I wasn't sure how that would be lived out. It was the fall of 2020, the world was in the midst of a pandemic as well as a spiritual and mental health crisis. While on retreat in the fierce desert landscape of west Texas, in Big Bend National Park, it came to me. There was no mechanism to bring the results of the research back to the Christian community. And conversely, the wider psychedelic community could benefit from the wisdom and knowledge of the contemplative and mystical tradition of Christianity, sadly lost to most Christians as well.

Ligare: A Christian Psychedelic Society was born. Since April 2021 we have been gathering Christians of all sorts and conditions. Not for experiences, since as of this writing these substances are still illegal in most of the world. We gather for education, community, and network building, resource sharing, and the work of preparing Christian leaders for a time in the not-too-distant future when the sacred substances will be more widely available and people will be looking for spiritual and religious communities in which to do the long-term work of healing and meaning making. In this work, I have returned to the roots of my own calling at the intersection of the church, Christianity, mental health, and healing.

In the book you are now holding, Dr. Ron Cole-Turner has given all of us interested in healing an invaluable resource. He brings his gifts as a theologian, teacher, writer, and pastor to this present moment: How might we engage the rich theological resources of the Christian church with these breakthrough treatments and experiences? How might our theology and our lives be changed through the powerful experiences of God these substances can occasion? The church has asked similar questions generation after generation and the answers build upon one another.

Cole-Turner offers an antidote to the fear and trepidation many Christians will have about these treatments, not so different from what the great twentieth-century theologian Karl Rahner, often quoted in this book, recognized in the reaction of some church leaders to the reforms of Vatican II. Rahner asks: "How different many things would be if we did not so often react to what is new with a self-assured superiority, an attitude of conservatism, adopted as a defence not of the honour of God and the teaching and institutions of the Church, but of our own selves, of what we have always been accustomed to."[1]

How different indeed! I believe we are on the cusp of a spiritual, religious, psychological, and medical reformation. It is coming in the nick of time. Only when the spiritual and the scientific truly come together will true healing happen. Frankly, the church can engage or get out of the way. Many, many Christians are hitching ourselves to engagement, and we desperately need solid scholarship and trusted theological resources like this to do it.

Thank you, Ron, for your commitment to the teaching and healing ministries of the church, and thank you dear reader for your courage, commitment, and faithfulness. Onward.

The Rev. Hunt Priest
Lent 2024
Savannah, Georgia

---

1. Rahner, "Do Not Stifle the Spirit!" 80.

Preface

In 2010, the transhumanists were at the peak of their influence. They were confident that the golden age of human enhancement technology was already dawning. Very soon, human beings will be smarter, faster, stronger, and more resistant to aging than ever before. The exuberance seemed a little excessive, but it made me wonder what Christianity had to say to a culture of transhumanism.

I started by making a list of human capacities that could be enhanced by technology such as pills, surgery, or implants. The most obvious use of performance-enhancing technology is in sports. Another target is intelligence, although so far coffee seems to work as well as anything. Longevity might be the most prized enhancement of all. If we can extend our lives by a few years, new technologies will come along to give us more extensions. Some of the transhumanists were talking about moral enhancement. They are afraid that morally unenhanced human beings were about to blow everything up. It turns out in fact that administering oxytocin can definitely give an empathy boost to humans or rodents alike. Making people more moral, however, is more complicated than just making them feel all cuddly.

What about spiritual enhancement through technology? I confess that on my list of human capacities that might be enhanced, I was overlooking what should have been most obvious to me. After all, at the time I was a teacher of theology at a seminary. Part of my job description was to think about spiritual enhancement.

My colleagues and I had regular lunchtime conversations about such things as spiritual formation for ministry. We floated many ideas, but we had no clear plan about how to help our students grow in their spiritual formation.

What if someone was working on a pill for spiritual enhancement? Having no idea what I might find, I started looking online and quickly discovered that human spiritual enhancement was a biomedical research project. The researchers referred to it as "mystical experiences," but that sounded close enough for me to keep reading. What I learned was that a research team led by Roland Griffiths at Johns Hopkins University School of Medicine, mindful of some of the psychedelic research from the sixties, was considering once again whether psychedelic experiences have spiritual significance.

Working in the research laboratories at Johns Hopkins, Griffiths and his team were testing a pill form of psilocybin, the key ingredient in sacred mushrooms. They enrolled healthy volunteers in a study to ask for evidence of a connection with spiritual experience. As I read on, it seemed to me that what they were doing was revolutionary in its significance for human spirituality and the future of religion. Their findings, published in a peer-reviewed science journal, seemed almost too amazing to be believable. Their 2006 paper ends with this paragraph:

> In conclusion, the present study showed that, when administered to volunteers under supportive conditions, psilocybin occasioned experiences similar to spontaneously occurring mystical experiences and which were evaluated by volunteers as having substantial and sustained personal meaning and spiritual significance. The ability to prospectively occasion mystical experiences should permit rigorous scientific investigations about their causes and consequences.[2]

Their numbers were really astounding. They claimed that "67% of the volunteers rated the experience with psilocybin to be either the single most meaningful experience of his or her life or

2. Griffiths et al., "Psilocybin Can Occasion," 282.

among the top five most meaningful experiences of his or her life."[3] Then came the clincher: "Based on a priori criteria, 22 of the total group of 36 volunteers had a 'complete' mystical experience after psilocybin."[4]

I read these statements, not knowing what was meant by a "complete" mystical experience but wondering whether any church service anywhere in the entire history of Christianity ever came close to being able to make comparable claims. I could not even remember someone coming out of church describing their experience at worship as one of the most meaningful of an entire lifetime. How could this be happening in a science lab if it never seems to happen in church?

Looking back, I see now that my first questions were a little silly. They nagged at me nonetheless, putting me at last on the path that led to this book. I read whatever I could find about biomedical research involving psychedelics. I attended conferences and talked with anyone who was interested in the spiritual dimensions of psychedelic experiences. My list of questions grew. How do we define mystical or spiritual experiences? How can psychedelics bring them about? What is the relationship between psychedelic spiritual experiences and their mental-health therapy applications?

Over time, my questions became increasingly theological. Psychedelics aside, what is the place of mystical or spiritual experiences in Christian theology? Why are they largely ignored in recent academic theology? Does Christianity have any place for spiritual experiences related to psychedelics?

As I learned about medical and scientific research involving psychedelics, I became more and more grateful to the people who make up the research teams. Because of their efforts, it is very likely that millions of people around the world who suffer from a wide range of mental health challenges will be offered what is now being called "psychedelic-assisted therapy." Some of the leaders in research, such as Roland Griffiths and William Richards,[5] are

3. Griffiths et al., "Psilocybin Can Occasion," 277.

4. Griffiths et al., "Psilocybin Can Occasion," 277.

5. Richards, *Sacred Knowledge.*

known to the public. Others work quietly and diligently out of the spotlight.

I am also grateful for the courage of church leaders who are beginning to speak publicly about the importance of psychedelic spiritual experiences and the possibility that they can be interpreted, not just as compatible with Christian faith, but as pathways to spiritual renewal. The network known as Ligare, founded in 2021 by the Rev. Hunt Priest, is especially noteworthy as the point of connection for Christian leaders working together to explore a Christian interpretation of psychedelic spiritual experiences. I am grateful to Hunt and to all the friends I have met through the Ligare network.

I must end this preface, however, with a disclaimer. Please know that this book is not intended as a substitute for professional medical advice, diagnosis, or treatment. No information in this book should be used to diagnose, treat, prevent, or cure any disease or condition. Readers are reminded that psychedelic substances are powerful and can cause challenging or difficult experiences with lasting consequences, and that their possession or use is illegal.

RON COLE-TURNER
MARCH 12, 2024

1

Psychedelics, Spiritual Experiences, and Christian Lives

EVER SINCE THE SIXTIES, people have claimed that psychedelics like LSD or psilocybin bring about intense subjective experiences that have mystical or spiritual qualities. Not always, of course, and not for everyone, but often enough to trigger a debate between advocates who thought these drugs have religious value and detractors who insisted they are dangerous to human health and social institutions.

Worries about the risks of psychedelics grew toward the end of the sixties. With the signing of the Controlled Substances Act in 1970, the United States became a leading player in a global campaign to stop the production and trade of a wide range of drugs, including cocaine and heroin. The Act created five schedules or classifications, with Schedule 1 as the most restrictive category, reserved for drugs that were thought to have a high potential for abuse and no known medical value. Psilocybin and LSD, along with many other drugs, were classified as Schedule 1 substances, making access to them illegal.

Enforcement was another matter, and the idea of a "war on drugs" was the political solution. It had popular support in the seventies and eighties, but law enforcement did not stop drug use so much as drive it underground. Through it all, a few guardians of the memories of the psychedelic sixties remained convinced that psilocybin and LSD simply do not belong in the same class as cocaine or heroin. Those who spoke up for access to psychedelics were quick to separate them from other drugs like cocaine, "crack," methamphetamine, and the newer synthetic opioids like fentanyl, which are addictive and dangerous. In the United States alone, over one hundred thousand people die each year from drug overdoses, with fentanyl involved in about two-thirds of this total.

Psychedelics do not pose the same sort of risks. Why, then, are they classified with other Schedule 1 drugs? Contrary to some of the war on drugs messages, psychedelics are not particularly dangerous for most users. According to the latest research, they do not have a high potential for addiction or abuse, but they do have clear medical uses. From university laboratories around the world, in research that is approved by governmental authorities and is published in peer-reviewed medical journals, mounting evidence directly contradicts the defining characteristics of Schedule 1.

Proof that psychedelics have important medical uses is now firmly established. Clinical trials are underway, and the first application for drug approval by the US Food and Drug Administration (FDA) was submitted in 2023 for review in 2024. Study after study points to the value of drugs like psilocybin or MDMA (commonly known as "ecstasy") to treat a range of mental health conditions, ranging from depression and post-traumatic stress disorder (PTSD) to substance abuse disorders and excessive anxiety when facing terminal illness. Far from being addictive, psychedelics are being used in clinical trials to treat addiction to substances like nicotine.

But the most surprising dimension of the new research is the rediscovery all over again of the spirituality connection. The idea that these drugs bring about spiritual or mystical experiences has been known for millennia in traditional or indigenous communities, who respected the healing powers of these substance and safeguarded their knowledge as they passed it from generation to generation. Psilocybin, present in many species of sacred mushrooms, was "discovered" in the fifties by outsiders. The news sparked widespread interest over the next two decades until the drugs were declared illegal. Today, the spirituality connection is back in front of us with greater clarity than ever before, and what we are learning about it is surprising even to the experts.

There are two distinct dimensions to the spirituality connection. First, psychedelics bring about spiritual or mystical experiences, at least for many users. Second, these same drugs have the potential to bring about mental health healing for many, arguably *because* they bring about intense spiritual experiences. In other words, psychedelics link to spiritual experiences, which link to mental health therapy. Interesting evidence suggests that psychedelics work best as treatments for mental health disorders when they bring about intense mystical or spiritual experiences. Much more needs to be learned about this two-dimensional connection, but the two-fold link between psychedelics, spiritual experience, and mental health therapy seems to be real.

How will church leaders and theological scholars react to the psychedelic spirituality connection? Some will ignore it, choosing instead to hold even more firmly to traditional Christian beliefs and practices, if not to an overt war-on-drugs worldview. Some will accept the idea that psychedelics may have mental health therapeutic benefits without it raising any theological curiosity about the link with spiritual experiences. Others will attack psychedelic spirituality as fakery or spiritual deviancy, maybe not exactly today's equivalent of sorcery but something along those lines. And some may fear that psychedelic spirituality is real and therefore a threat to traditional religion because it is a more readily accessible and reliable path to spiritual growth than anything offered by churches.

And then perhaps there are some of us who, while remaining convinced that the core message of the scriptures has enduring value in every age, will ask whether Christian spirituality can be compatible with psychedelic spirituality. Not every Christian should use psychedelics, and not everyone who uses psychedelics for spiritual purposes should warm to Christianity. But for some of us at least, perhaps the two can overlap, with Christian faith providing an overarching context for our multifaceted spiritual lives in which a host of experiences, including some with psychedelics, can bring us to moments of holiness, awe, and healing.

A PSYCHEDELIC RENAISSANCE?

The new world of psychedelics is an increasingly busy space, with back-to-back conferences, research publications, news reports, best-selling books turned into Netflix specials, and millions of dollars in philanthropic funding and private venture capital, all building expectations that at least some of these drugs will soon be approved for mental health therapy before 2030.

Major universities and corporate research laboratories are leading the way in research, and their findings are reported in established, peer-reviewed journals or showing up in patent applications. Mounting evidence shows that these drugs have therapeutic benefits in treating a range of mental health conditions, from depression to PTSD to substance addictions. Multi-million-dollar psychedelic research centers are popping up at universities especially in the United States, and clinical trials involving psychedelics are underway around the world. Some are calling it the "psychedelic renaissance," this head-spinning and fast-moving mix of biomedical research, boom-and-bust IPOs, media hype, and drug decriminalization.

Despite the pace, most of the psychedelic pharmaceutical research is still in the early stages, perhaps phase 1 or 2 of clinical trials. Early results are so promising that twice now, the US FDA has granted breakthrough therapy status to expedite the complicated process of getting approval and funding for research involving illegal substances.

One breakthrough candidate is MDMA. The drug was vilified during the war on drugs as a dangerous party drug. In 2024, however, the FDA agreed to review a new drug application for the use of MDMA in capsule form in use with psychotherapy for the treatment of PTSD. The review was given priority review status.

The application was turned down by the FDA, but new applications will be submitted.

Psilocybin has also been designated as a breakthrough therapy drug by the FDA, first in 2018 and again in 2019. In early trials, psilocybin has shown surprising effectiveness in helping patients deal with depression, and the benefits from one or two sessions seem to last for months at least, possibly longer. Once FDA approval is granted for even one psychedelic drug, many expect the pressure to build to remove some psychedelics from the list of Schedule 1 substances, along with efforts to decriminalize possession for personal use.

The promising future of pharmaceutical research involving psychedelics is the main reason why some call this moment the psychedelic renaissance. Growing confidence that psychedelic-assisted therapy is the next big thing in mental health is attracting private capital. It also provides a powerful argument in the effort to decriminalize access to these drugs, whose Schedule 1 classification is based on their potential for abuse and their lack of medical benefit, claims that are contradicted by today's scientific research. Localized decriminalization is a complicated process in the United States because federal law makes possession and use of these drugs illegal everywhere. Even so, local organizers have succeeded in changing the ways in which enforcement occurs. In cities like Denver, Oakland, Washington, DC, Detroit, and Seattle, as well as states like Oregon and Colorado, police enforcement is assigned a low priority, effectively meaning that possessing and sharing small amounts of plant-based psychedelics is permitted.

The very notion of a psychedelic renaissance is offensive to those who point to the long history of the use of some of these substances in indigenous communities around the world. From their perspective, after colonial powers tried but failed to suppress the use of psychedelics, they are now congratulating themselves today on having discovered how to exploit the mystical and medicinal powers they once feared. The best-known example is the use of psilocybin by various groups throughout what is now Mexico. The first European report of psychedelic mushrooms dates to 1530, when the Franciscan friar Bernardino de Sahagún reported from New Spain that the people they encountered "ate these little mushrooms with honey, and when they began to be excited by them, they began to dance, some singing, others weeping, for they were already intoxicated by mushrooms. Some did not want to sing but sat down in their quarters and remained there as if in a meditative mood. Some saw themselves dying in a vision and wept."[1] From the start, Spanish colonial and religious authorities tried to prohibit the use of mushrooms "as part of broader efforts to suppress Indigenous religious, medicinal, and cultural practices." Despite their efforts, "use of psilocybin mushrooms nevertheless continued to exist among different Indigenous groups despite Spanish colonial prohibition."[2]

In the fifties, these mushrooms were "discovered" by the husband-and-wife team of R. Gordon Wasson and Valentina Pavlovna Wasson, who located their use in Mexico and published the results in 1957. An article in *Life* magazine by Gordon Wasson included photos and was seen by millions of Americans.[3] The local healer who shared the ceremony with Wasson was "severely impacted." She was "stigmatized in her community for the dramatic changes Wasson's publications precipitated in Huautla de Jiménez, which became a countercultural pilgrimage destination for mid-1960s hippies in pursuit of 'magic mushrooms.'"[4]

In Brazil and throughout the Amazon region, traditional groups use ayahuasca, which contains dimethyltryptamine or DMT, for religious ceremonies. About a century ago, ayahuasca use was fused with elements of Christianity and African religions to form a new religious movement known as Santo Daime. The religion has spread to other countries, including the United States, where it is also known as the União do Vegetal. Outside these churches the use of ayahuasca is legally prohibited, but its ceremonial use is protected in the United States under the Religious

1. Spiers et al., "Indigenous Psilocybin Mushroom Practices," 2.
2. Spiers et al., "Indigenous Psilocybin Mushroom Practices," 2.
3. Wasson, "Seeking the Magic Mushroom."
4. Spiers et al., "Indigenous Psilocybin Mushroom Practices," 4.

Freedom Restoration Act of 1993. Similar legal protection exists for the Native American Church for the use of peyote, which contains mescaline.

Despite these protections, the history of colonialism and exploitation hangs over the entire field of psychedelic research. Christianity played a role in the suppression of traditional religious practices by providing a theological condemnation of psychedelic use. Avoiding the mistakes of the past is a major concern facing anyone who supports the idea that these substances can be beneficial, either medically or spiritually. The Chacruna Institute on Psychedelic Plant Medicines provides helpful resources, including an edited collection of essays entitled *Psychedelic Justice*.[5]

Another problem involving the rhetoric of renaissance is that it is vulnerable to hype, which exaggerates the benefits of psychedelics while downplaying the risks. Pushing back against the claim that psychedelics are addictive and medically dangerous, early researchers were understandably eager to prove the opposite. As we come closer to the time of FDA approval, however, the climate has shifted. It is widely agreed now that careful attention to the risks of psychedelics is the best path to their approval and use. Today's researchers agree that we must ask how frequently the users of psychedelics have what are called "challenging experiences." What makes them challenging, and what problems linger after the drug's activity has worn off? Are the problems always manageable when psychedelics are used in a clinical setting as part of psychedelic-assisted therapy? Are problems more common when people use psychedelics on their own? And if so, what do people need to know about the risks involved or about how to manage them?

WHAT ARE PSYCHEDELICS?

The word "psychedelic" was coined in 1956 by Humphrey Osmond, who was one of the first people to study the medical value of LSD.

---

5. Labate and Cavnar, *Psychedelic Justice*.

In a letter to Aldous Huxley, Osmond invents the word as part of a simple rhyme: "To fathom Hell or soar angelic, Just take a pinch of psychedelic."[6] The meaning of "psychedelic" is usually explained in terms of its Greek roots, and "mind-manifesting" is the most common English equivalent.

Our focus here in this book is mostly on what researchers today call "classic psychedelics." The two most widely known classic psychedelics are psilocybin and LSD. Psilocybin is the active compound in what are often called magic or sacred mushrooms. LSD (lysergic acid diethylamide) was synthesized in the laboratory by Albert Hofmann, a Swiss chemist, in 1943. Other classic psychedelics include DMT (dimethyltryptamine), found in the South American sacramental beverage ayahuasca. Another is mescaline, the main psychoactive agent in peyote. Except for LSD, these substances are found in nature. Chemists have isolated and studied them, along with variants or analogs that have been created in the lab.

In addition to the classic psychedelics, there are other substances that are sometimes grouped together because they have similar effects. One example is MDMA (methylenedioxymethamphetamine) or ecstasy. Its subjective effects are broadly similar to classic psychedelics. Classic psychedelics, however, act in the brain mainly by binding to serotonin receptor sites, specifically the serotonin 2A receptor (5-HT2AR). MDMA's action in the brain is slightly different. Rather than binding to serotonin receptor sites, MDMA appears to work by triggering the sudden release of the brain's own serotonin.[7] Despite this important technical difference, MDMA figures prominently in today's psychedelic biomedical research. Even though it is not a classic psychedelic strictly speaking, MDMA is included here.

So is ketamine, which is even more of an outlier than MDMA in terms of its effects on the brain. It is used medically as an anesthetic but with known hallucinogenic effects. We also include ibogaine, which is derived from the root of a plant that is known

6. Grob and Bravo, "High Road," 7.

7. Johnson et al., "Classic Psychedelics," 84.

and used in traditional communities in central Africa. While our focus here is centered mainly on the classic psychedelics, it makes sense to include these other substances like MDMA, ketamine, and ibogaine. All are known to have similar effects on the brain, even though they act through different pathways. We will group them together based on what they do, not on how they do it.[8] All of them have captured the attention of biomedical researchers, who are studying their various properties in search of slightly different approaches to psychedelic medicine. And perhaps the most compelling reason to include them here is that they are all illegal under most circumstances. They are all on the list of Schedule 1 drugs as defined in the United States by the Controlled Substances Act.

Psychedelics are sometimes called "hallucinogens" or "hallucinogenic drugs." Often the word "hallucinogen" is used simply as a legacy term based on the idea that as a group, these drugs bring about altered states of consciousness. More often today, the term is being pushed aside in favor of "psychedelics." According to one group of experts, "the term 'hallucinogen,' which has been widely applied to classic psychedelics in scientific circles, is not ideal because these substances do not typically produce frank hallucinations, and this term, which connotes only perceptual effects, is an insufficient description of the often-radical effects these drugs have on human consciousness and one's sense of self. Therefore, the term 'hallucinogen' has fallen out of favor, with a re-emergence of the scientific use of the term 'psychedelic' to refer to these substances."[9] For these reasons, we avoid using the word "hallucinogenic" because it brings up the one thing that some people fear most about these drugs. Is the primary effect of these drugs to generate delusions or hallucinations? If so, then it would make sense to avoid them altogether.

We also avoid using the word "entheogens." In some ways, the words hallucinogens and entheogens are rhetorical or semantic opposites. "Hallucinogens" embeds a criticism of these drugs in

8. Mitchell and Anderson, "Psychedelic Therapies Reconsidered," 1–2.

9. Johnson et al., "Classic Psychedelics," 84.

their name while using the word "entheogens" commends them. It points to their spiritual or mystical dimensions by suggesting that the drugs help people experience or encounter the divine that is within them. It is true of course that these drugs can be used for spiritual purposes and with powerful spiritual results. When that happens, it may make sense to call them entheogens. But the drugs have other functions and uses, and so we avoid using the word "entheogen" as the general term for these substances.

Some prefer to speak of these substances as "plant medicines" or "spirit medicines." One practical advantage of calling them "plant medicines" is to build popular support for ballot measures aimed at decriminalization. Voters seem willing if not eager to decriminalize nature, and campaigns that use this slogan have been successful in cities across America. LSD, of course, is not based on a plant or a fungus, and so it is left out when a public campaign is defined as having to do with nature.

When it comes to public perceptions, it matters very much what we call these drugs. To refer to them as hallucinogens suggests that their main effect is to bring about worrisome delusions. To call them entheogens goes too far in the opposite direction by suggesting that these drugs have the power to remove illusions by revealing what is truly divine. To call them "plant medicines" suggests that they are benignly natural.

Here we use the word "psychedelics," not a perfect word and far from neutral in its rhetorical weight, especially in its association with the counterculture of the sixties and seventies. But for that reason, it retains a certain edginess, a constant reminder of the once-forbidden territory that now must be explored with care and open-mindedness. Above all, the word "psychedelic" seems right because it keeps us in a neutral zone between hallucinogens and entheogens. By using it, we avoid dismissing the spiritual as delusional but also stay clear of preloading unproven theological claims into our choice of words. The question of the religious or spiritual interpretation of psychedelics is an open question.

THE SPIRITUALITY CONNECTION

What is beyond question, however, is that many people who use psychedelics report that these drugs do in fact bring about an experience that they hold to be profoundly meaningful or spiritual. It is equally clear based on biomedical research that many people have found significant and lasting help in dealing with mental health concerns through psychedelic-assisted therapy. How can we understand the connection between psychedelics and spiritual experiences? And what are we to think about an apparent connection between psychedelic spiritual or mystical experiences and psychedelic therapy?

Anyone who wants to study the psychedelic/spirituality connection must first define terms like "mystical experience" or "spiritual experience." For scientists, the challenge is not just to define the terms but to find a way to measure them. How is it possible to define something as broad or vague as mystical experience? What indicators suggest that it has occurred, especially in a laboratory setting?

To get a definitional handle on mystical experience, researchers have found guidance in the writings of William James (1842–1910) and W. T. Stace (1886–1967). The properties or features of mysticism described in Stace's *Mysticism and Philosophy* (1960) became the basis for trying to quantify the mystical or spiritual qualities or features of psychedelic experiences in the lab. Using measurements derived from Stace, researchers have found consistently that there is a reliable link between psychedelics and quantifiable mystical-type experience. In 2006, at the dawn of today's psychedelic renaissance, researchers at Johns Hopkins University published evidence to support the claim that "Psilocybin can occasion mystical-type experiences having substantial and sustained personal meaning and spiritual significance," to quote the lengthy title of the report.[10]

The 2006 report is significant for two reasons. First, it provides the kind of evidence we expect to see in medical research, in this case not to show that a particular drug is effective in treating a

---

10. Griffiths et al., "Psilocybin Can Occasion," 268.

disease but to show that it "occasions" or brings about an experience with mystical qualities. For many people, this alone was a breakthrough, the first medically rigorous "proof" of what had been widely reported anecdotally.

The second significant point made in the 2006 report is that psilocybin can generate experiences with mystical qualities almost on command, bringing them about reliably and predictably in a research laboratory. As a scientific claim, this is something utterly new in the entire history of human spiritual experience. What it means is that with the help of research volunteers, scientists now can look at experiences of a mystical nature from a wholly different point of view, objectively as it were, or from the outside of the brain looking in. By administering these drugs in a laboratory setting, researchers can use brain imaging to study human spiritual experience in the brain. They can watch it while it is occurring.

When the power of psychedelics to bring about mystical experiences meets the imaging capacities of technology in the research laboratory, the brains of human beings can be observed for the first time *while they are having mystical-like experiences.* One immediate challenge is knowing how to correlate brain imaging data with the subjective or phenomenological reports of the research volunteers. But even bigger challenges lie ahead, as scientists debate what brain imaging suggests about how psychedelics actually work in the brain therapeutically and mystically. How are the two aspects, the therapeutic and the mystical, connected in the complex processes of brain and mind? How far will psychedelics take science in helping us understand the mysteries of personhood, consciousness, and altered states of awareness?

Is it possible for theology to learn something new from today's psychedelic science? Getting at that question involves detailed attention to psychedelic research. But it also forces us to take another look at Christianity's traditional ideas about mysticism and spiritual experiences. What we find is that all too often, traditional theology has pushed spiritual experience to the side as unimportant. It is portrayed as mere subjectivity and therefore as something wholly unreliable as a basis for theological insight. It may be important for individuals, but it is an untrustworthy and unusable source for theology.

Marginalization of the mystical has been a hallmark of modern theology. Perhaps today's psychedelic research will change that. Mystical experience is now front-page news in a way that traditional Christianity cannot ignore easily. Science-based theological questions and challenges keep piling up. For example, what does psychedelic-assisted mental health therapy suggest in general about the place of spirituality in mental health? What does psychedelic neuroscience imply about the capacity of the human brain for mystical experiences? Can psychedelic spirituality and Christian spirituality go hand in hand, not as identical to each other but somehow complementing each other? Will Christianity offer support and validation for psychedelic mystical experiences? Will Christian leaders provide encouragement for anyone wishing to integrate a drug-related mystical experience into the complex narrative of a Christian life?

The search for even tentative answers to these questions is a marker of the adequacy of Christianity's response to today's culture. But more than that, the spiritual well-being of many thousands of individual Christians depends on finding meaningful answers.

If the spiritual lives of individual Christians are affected by our search for answers to these questions, so also is our broader culture's shared assessment. In the decades just ahead, what will be said of the responses of churches to the growing use of psychedelics for mental health and spiritual experience? There is no guarantee that today's psychedelic renaissance will necessarily go well as a process of cultural transformation. Will it lead to a growing collective appreciation that spiritual wholeness and personal enrichment are good things that can be attained by ordinary people? Will it bring new therapies that are truly healing? Will it enrich our humanity and open new pathways of human flourishing?

IT CAN ALL GO WRONG AGAIN

In the fifties and sixties, LSD and psilocybin were available legally. Many people used them for personal growth, self-discovery, or spiritual experiences. Scientists in various disciplines used them as tools of research. "In fact, the range of researchers was remarkable and included psychologists and psychiatrists, biologists and pharmacologists, sociologists and anthropologists, philosophers and theologians, as well as laboratory and clinical scientists," according to one summary. "In the short span of a decade and a half, they produced thousands of research articles and dozens of books."[11]

By and large, Christian scholars and leaders in the sixties did not address the spiritual significance of psychedelics. One prominent exception was Huston Smith, who pleaded for serious, mainstream attention to the spiritual potential of these drugs. Widely seen as a leading expert on world religions, Smith became interested in psychedelics after reading Aldous Huxley's *The Doors of Perception* (1954). Huxley joined Smith for a semester at the Massachusetts Institute of Technology, and together they connected in 1960 with Timothy Leary and the "Center for Personality Research" at Harvard University. In 1962, Smith was part of the famous Good Friday Marsh Chapel Experiment organized by Walter Pahnke, in which twenty theological students participated in a double-blind session with psilocybin.[12] The next year, in 1963, Smith published what is to this day the most widely reprinted essay ever to appear in the *American Journal of Philosophy*, entitled "Do Drugs Have Religious Import?"[13]

Despite the efforts by Smith and a few others, public opinion at the end of the sixties became increasingly hostile to drug use, regardless of whether it was for spiritual exploration or scientific research. The political dynamics of the time led eventually to the Controlled Substances Act of 1970. Access to drugs was so tightly restricted that even clinical research was banned.

11. Smith, "Do Drugs Have Religious Import?" 223.

12. Doblin, "Pahnke's 'Good Friday Experiment.'"

13. Smith, "Do Drugs Have Religious Import?" 223.

Many versions of what happened with psychedelics in the sixties and seventies have been written, and there is no shortage of explanations about what went wrong. At the beginning of the sixties, interest in psychedelics was strong and widespread. Support, however, was strongest outside the leading cultural institutions of the time, including the religious establishment. The value of psychedelic spirituality was not accepted by traditional religious institutions in the United States, largely dominated as they were by mainstream Protestants. While flourishing outside this mainstream, psychedelics became associated chiefly with what was called "recreational use," a term that still has the effect of trivializing their potential and undermining their acceptance.

Rick Doblin, who deserves credit for having done more than anyone else to bring about today's psychedelic renaissance, believes that what went wrong in the sixties and seventies was that these drugs were seen not just as recreational but as countercultural. "The flaw of the early psychedelic movement was that they made it countercultural, a revolution," Doblin told the *Washington Post* in 2017. He is determined not to let that happen again to the psychedelic renaissance, partly by encouraging biomedical research published in established science journals. "Culture is dominant. Culture is always going to win," he said.[14]

When asked in 2005 for his opinion on what went wrong in the sixties and seventies, Huston Smith pointed to the failure of religious institutions and scholars to create what he called "a religious context." One reason "many ideals were not achieved may have been due to context, or the lack thereof. By ignoring the religious context for these substances, one failed to create genuinely holy experiences."[15]

Could it all go wrong again? Could today's psychedelic renewal meet the same fate as the previous psychedelic era of the 1960s? While it is hard to imagine that the momentum for change could be completely reversed, it is easy to think of new ways in which things could go terribly wrong. For example, one risk is that

14. Wan, "Ecstasy Could Be 'Breakthrough,'" para. 22.

15. Smith, "Do Drugs Have Religious Import?" 232.

premature decriminalization will lead to overly casual use, with possible harm to individuals. Every expert in the field insists that psychedelics are potent substances that need care if they are to be used safely. Just how should decriminalization be rolled out, and what precautions should be in place as that happens?

So-called "bad trips" or difficult journeys are always possible. Warnings about the dangers of bad trips may have been exaggerated in the war on drugs rhetoric, but the phenomenon is real and should be taken seriously. Often it is said that even a bad trip can have a good outcome, and there is no doubt that a difficult or emotionally painful drug session can in the end lead to new insight and healing. But that is not always the case. The possibility that new mental health problems will occur cannot be dismissed altogether, even though this is only a remote possibility when careful screening and session planning are in place. According to a leading team of researchers, "Some of the perceived harms of psychedelics—for example, that they lead to addiction and are neurotoxic—are largely refuted by research of the past decades. Other risks, such as the risks of psychotic episodes or overdose, are rare and only reported in individual cases, but these risks still need to be minimized by careful patient selection and preparation. The past decade of research and clinical experience has increasingly demonstrated how psychedelics can be used safely under medical supervision, and safe use guidelines are progressively well defined."[16]

Anyone using psychedelics, regardless of the context or the intent, should be advised about the risks and should take reasonable precautions. Things can go wrong for individuals. Drugs like psilocybin remain illegal in the US, and anyone thinking about using them should know that despite growing cultural tolerance and campaigns toward decriminalization, the number of seizures of illegal drugs by law enforcement is going up in the US, from 402 seizures in 2017 to 1,396 in 2022.[17]

16. Schlag et al., "Adverse Effects," 11.

17. Palamar et al., "National and Regional Trends," 1.

Even more worrisome, however, are the ways in which things can go wrong for patients in our institutions and healthcare systems. Many doubt that our systems will be ready to meet the needs of patients if psychedelic-assisted mental health therapy is approved by regulatory authorities. Psychedelic-assisted therapy is likely to be sought by hundreds of thousands if not millions of people who experience the conditions that may be treatable. As promising as psychedelic-assisted therapy may be, experts in this area of research are clear that the psychedelic drugs play only a supportive role in the healing process. They are not to be used without the support of trained therapists with broad experience in psychotherapy and specialized training in psychedelic-assisted therapy. It is not clear how the demand for these therapists will be met in the future, or whether medical insurance will cover the costs even in part.

The psychedelic/spirituality connection noted earlier complicates these problems even more. It is not known whether psychedelic-assisted health therapy works best when the patient undergoes something like a spiritual or mystical experience in the course of therapy. Even if the spiritual experience seems largely coincidental and not necessary, the fact that it occurs at all with some level of frequency raises important questions. Are patients in secular mental health settings expected to move through psychedelic-assisted therapy without spiritual support? Are people trained in psychedelic-assisted therapy expected to provide spiritual help, or will chaplains be added to the healing team for use as requested?

As research goes forward, drug companies old and new are trying to find ways to benefit from the use of medical psychedelics. Patent applications are being filed for treatment protocols and drug formula variants, and patent approvals are being granted in the United States and elsewhere. No one knows yet just how much the field will be commercialized or how costs will be managed, but there are risks that therapies might be approved but not accessible to those who need them, or that opportunities for personal or spiritual growth in a well-staffed retreat setting might cost more than most people can afford.

The risk that should concern us most, however, is that many people will have intense and meaningful spiritual experiences, but they will not be given support and encouragement as they go through the long process of integrating their experiences into their lives. Secular institutions, no matter how well intended and staffed, can only do so much to help people who want to connect their psychedelic experiences with their Christian commitments. Christian leaders and churches are needed to provide the kind of spiritual support we hope to see, but how many of them will ignore the challenge or fail to acknowledge the authentic spiritual potential of psychedelics?

As individuals make their way through intense psychedelic experiences, whether challenging or blissful, many will want to connect the meaning of their experiences with the meaning of their faith. A church unprepared, led by clergy who ignore or dismiss the authenticity or the significance of psychedelic spiritual experiences, will fail to meet the needs of a whole new class of spiritual seekers.

The purpose of this book is to invite Christian leaders to understand the spiritual challenges of psychedelic drugs and to work together to prepare the church to meet the emerging need for spiritual care. Chapter 2 begins with a summary of what we are learning about psychedelics and mental health, and chapter 3 explores the question about the multiple levels of psychedelic action in the human body and brain. In chapter 4, we consider what the scientific study of psychedelics can reveal about spiritual experiences in general. In chapter 5, we turn to questions about the meaning of mystical and spiritual experiences in the history of Christianity, while chapter 6 suggests how a Christian theology of spiritual experience can take note of psychedelics. Finally, chapter 7 considers the public and pastoral role of the church in creating a spiritual home that welcomes those with psychedelic spiritual experiences who want to integrate their experience with Christian faith.

Our vision is that as psychedelic mystical experiences become more common, anyone who seeks spiritual support will find it widely available within the context of Christianity. Some may be just starting to think seriously about whether to take a psychedelic journey. Others may be actively preparing for one. Some may already be reflecting on what happened to them spiritually in their experience. At every stage, spiritual help should be offered to all who seek it. No one should be told that psychedelic spirituality is anti-Christian or that they must choose between their experiences and their faith.

Thinking more broadly beyond the help that might be provided to individuals, it is our intention to help create a cultural environment that values the spiritual dimension of psychedelic experiences. The public voice of the church should encourage our wider society to appreciate the power of psychedelics as a pathway to spirituality. Others are already at work using medical research to create a cultural environment in which most people will agree that psychedelic drugs can be used as new pathways toward mental health therapy. It is up to us in religious institutions to promote an environment in which people will agree that psychedelic drugs can provide moments of spiritual experience and can lead to lives that are spiritually transformed.

2

Psychedelics and Healing

WILL PSYCHEDELIC DRUGS PROVE to be the next big advance in mental health therapy? It is not just the researchers and their investors who have high hopes. Would-be patients are eager for new treatment options. When one team invited volunteers to apply for a study with one hundred openings, they were shocked when 15,000 people tried to sign up.[1]

Whether such high hopes can really be translated into effective, affordable, and deliverable treatments is still an open question. The range of conditions currently under study using psychedelics includes post-traumatic stress disorder (PTSD), major depression disorder (MDD), obsessive-compulsive disorder (OCD), depression in bipolar 2 disorder, eating disorders such as anorexia nervosa and bulimia nervosa, fibromyalgia, phantom limb pain, migraine and cluster headaches, concussion headaches, "existential distress" associated with serious medical illness, and substance disorders involving smoking, alcohol, methamphetamine use, and cocaine use disorder.[2] Anyone concerned about the global state of mental health today is more than ready for a new approach to any one of these conditions. Here in this chapter, we will take a closer

1. Eisenstein, "Psychedelic Escape," 89.
2. Mitchell and Anderson, "Psychedelic Therapies Reconsidered."

look at biomedical research into the use of psychedelics in mental health therapy.

Even if it were true that psychedelics only had significance for mental health therapy, that in itself would be reason enough for religious leaders to pay attention and to offer encouragement. In fact, psychedelics do much more than help address certain mental health conditions. They also bring on spiritual experiences that are intense, meaningful, and theologically significant in ways that go far beyond their mental health benefits. More than that, there is strong evidence for a link between the mental health therapeutic benefit and the intensity of the spiritual experience. We are just beginning to understand the complex connections between psychedelics, mental health, and spiritual experiences. This chapter focuses on the link with mental health, and later chapters turn to questions of spiritual experience.

PSYCHEDELICS AND POST-TRAUMATIC STRESS DISORDER

Can psychedelics contribute to mental health therapy for conditions like PTSD? The idea has been around for a long time, not just since the decades of the sixties but over millennia as part of indigenous cultural traditions around the world. Does the idea meet the standards of evidence required today in the context of advanced medicine? Researchers think that the answer is yes, and growing evidence supports their view that psychedelics can be part of safe and effective treatment protocols for a wide range of mental health conditions.

The idea of psychedelic-assisted therapy is still taking shape in mental health research settings. The concept is fairly simple. In the context of psychotherapy, a patient is offered one or more treatment sessions using a psychedelic compound, such as psilocybin or MDMA. Starting with the standard treatment protocol, researchers make modifications in order to try to get the most benefit from the use of psychedelic drugs. In addition to the drug experience, this means adding "a preparation period prior to the dosing session and an integration period afterwards, in order to maximize the therapeutic value and minimize challenges related to the experience. Preparation includes setting an intention, receiving psycho-education, practicing coping skills, and building rapport with the facilitators."[3] The general idea of psychedelic-assisted therapy is being tested with several different psychedelic substances in an effort to treat a wide range of mental health challenges. Psychedelic-assisted therapy protocols vary because mental health experts hold different views on the best form of psychotherapy. Staffing and training requirements also vary from one study center to another.

In order to know whether psychedelic-assisted therapy is worth pursuing, researchers have to ask whether the use of psychedelics adds something of value to the existing treatment. If talk therapy is at least partly effective in treating depression, does the use of psychedelics make talk therapy more effective? This is the logic of psychedelic-assisted therapy research. Psychedelics are not typically being studied as stand-alone treatments but as supplements to an established therapeutic process. When psychedelics are added to the treatment, do they make a worthwhile difference? If so, in what ways might they also complicate the process in terms of staffing or costs? What effect does the use of psychedelics have on the process of informed consent? Many questions are still unanswered. The FDA, however, may approve a proposal for psychedelic-assisted therapy to treat PTSD within a few years, with more approvals likely to follow.

According to government data, suicide claimed the lives of 6,261 US service veterans in 2019, a rate of seventeen per day.[4] Post-traumatic stress disorder is commonly seen as a major cause. Combat veterans who served in Afghanistan and Iraq are especially vulnerable, with 16 percent of them having been diagnosed with PTSD.[5] When the Veterans Administration provides therapy, it usually involves "prolonged exposure therapy" and "cognitive

---

3. Peacock et al., "Spiritual Health Practitioners' Contributions," 2.

4. Londoño, "After Six-Decade Hiatus," A14.

5. Londoño, "After Six-Decade Hiatus," A14.

processing therapy" that require patients to revisit and reframe their negative thoughts. Anti-anxiety drugs and antidepressants are also used, but the combined result has not provided the help that is needed.[6]

PTSD is not limited to combat veterans. Police and other first responders are also highly vulnerable. It is commonly estimated that at some point in their lives, one out of twenty Americans meet the diagnostic criteria for PTSD. Women are more likely to suffer from PTSD than men (8 percent compared to 4 percent).

When early studies showed that MDMA can treat PTSD in 2017, the FDA labelled MDMA a "breakthrough therapy." That opened the pathway for more research, funded in part by the Multidisciplinary Association for Psychedelic Studies (MAPS), a nonprofit organization that supports biomedical research involving psychedelics through a public benefit corporation. Late in 2023, MAPS reorganized its public benefit corporation as Lykos Therapeutics in order to tap more funding and personnel resources. Working in cooperation with the Veterans Administration, MAPS-funded researchers worked at various sites across the US. They recruited an ethnically and racially diverse group of carefully screened volunteers. The treatment process combined conventional group therapy with three MDMA treatments, each roughly a month apart.[7]

More results were published in 2021, with a follow-up in 2023. Keep in mind that everyone in the trial received the same conventional therapy, which despite its inadequacies is not wholly ineffective. What researchers wanted to know is whether the MDMA sessions made a significant difference for those suffering from PTSD. The report concluded that it did, claiming that MDMA "significantly improved PTSD symptoms and functional impairment . . . compared to placebo with therapy over 18 weeks."[8] With these results in hand, MAPS submitted a new drug application to the FDA at the end of 2023.

6. Londoño, "After Six-Decade Hiatus," A14.

7. Mitchell et al., "MDMA-Assisted Therapy."

8. Mitchell et al., "MDMA-Assisted Therapy," 2477.

The 2023 report calls attention to the fact that the participants were "ethnoracially diverse." One reason why diversity is especially important when it comes to PTSD is because of disparities in exposure to trauma. "Due to disparities in trauma exposure, gender-diverse and transgender individuals, ethnoracial minorities, first responders, military personnel, veterans and victims of chronic sexual abuse have a disproportionately higher risk of developing PTSD." Despite a higher risk of exposure, the researchers note, "diverse populations are historically underrepresented in clinical trials."[9]

For some, traumatic experiences are accompanied by physical trauma to the brain, a condition known as "traumatic brain injury" or TBI. In 2024 it was reported that a psychedelic drug called ibogaine may prove effective as a treatment for special forces combat veterans suffering from TBI. According to the report, "participants showed a remarkable reduction in these symptoms . . . and the benefits were sustained at the 1-month follow-up," when the pilot study ended. The research team claims that their study offers evidence that ibogaine could be part of "a powerful therapeutic for the transdiagnostic psychiatric symptoms that can emerge after TBI and repeated exposure to blasts and combat, including suicidality."[10]

PSYCHEDELIC-ASSISTED THERAPY AND DEPRESSION

The US National Institute of Mental Health (NIMH) estimates that 14.5 million or 5.7 percent of all American adults had at least one major depressive episode "with severe impairment" in 2021.[11] NIMH defines a major depressive episode as "a period of at least two weeks when a person experienced a depressed mood or loss of interest or pleasure in daily activities, and had a majority of

---

9. Mitchell et al., "MDMA-Assisted Therapy," 2474.

10. Cherian et al., "Magnesium-Ibogaine Therapy," 379.

11. "Major Depression," paras. 8–10.

specified symptoms, such as problems with sleep, eating, energy, concentration, or self-worth."[12] Women suffered a major depressive episode more often than men (10.3 percent compared to 6.2 percent). Young adults were especially vulnerable. For those between 18–25 years of age, the prevalence rate was an astounding 18.6 percent.[13] Worldwide, major depressive disorder (MDD) affects somewhere between 280 and 300 million individuals. It is "the number one cause of disability," and those with MDD are 1.7 times more likely than others to die of all causes.[14]

When it is available, mental health treatment for depression usually relies on some form of talk therapy, often combined with prescription drugs such as selective serotonin reuptake inhibitors (SSRIs). Treatment, however, is not always helpful. Some experts have begun to use the term "treatment-resistant depression" (TRD) to refer to major depression "that does not respond to two or more adequate antidepressant trials, or a relapse or recurrence of a major depressive episode during treatment." Some estimate that "TRD affects up to a third of all individuals with major depressive disorder."[15] Others estimate that "approximately 30% of individuals suffering with TRD attempt suicide at least once in their lifetime."[16]

Faced with numbers like that, mental health experts are eager to find new treatments, and many of them see psychedelic-assisted psychotherapy as the most promising new approach. Reporting their findings from a major randomized clinical trial, one team of researchers claimed that their results "demonstrated the efficacy of psilocybin-assisted therapy in producing large, rapid, and sustained antidepressant effects among patients with MDD. These data expand the findings of previous studies involving patients with cancer and depression as well as patients with treatment-resistant

12. "Major Depression," para. 4.

13. "Major Depression," paras. 10–15.

14. Davis et al., "Effects of Psilocybin-Assisted Therapy," 482.

15. Husain et al., "Psilocybin for Treatment-Resistant Depression," 1.

16. Husain et al., "Psilocybin for Treatment-Resistant Depression," 1.

depression by suggesting that psilocybin may be effective in the much larger population of MDD."[17]

When they reassessed the mental health of their original research volunteers one year later, researchers found that the benefits of psilocybin were still present. They claim that their finding "suggests that two doses of psilocybin provided in the context of supportive therapy for MDD produced large and stable antidepressant effects throughout a 12-month follow-up period." When they re-evaluated their volunteers at quarterly intervals over the following year, they found that measurements of depression "decreased substantially after treatment and remained low."[18] In 2023, based on a larger study with a more diverse group of volunteers, researchers made this claim in their report: "Psilocybin treatment was associated with a clinically significant sustained reduction in depressive symptoms and functional disability, without serious adverse events. These findings add to increasing evidence that psilocybin—when administered with psychological support—may hold promise as a novel intervention for MDD."[19] Pointing to reports like this, experts predict that FDA approval for psychedelic-assisted therapy in the treatment of depression may come by the end of the decade.

Until then, however, another drug that is sometimes grouped together with psychedelics is already approved and being used to treat depression. Ketamine, first synthesized in the sixties, is a Schedule III drug. The FDA has approved its use as a general anesthetic, making it available for so-called "off-label" use, mainly as a treatment option for depression, even though the FDA has not approved of this use. A modified form of ketamine, known as esketamine and sold as Spravato in the form of a nasal spray, was approved by the FDA in 2019 as an alternative for therapy for major, treatment-resistant depression. In 2023, however, the FDA issued a warning to the public about the risks of using esketamine, especially when it is ordered online and used at home.

17. Davis et al., "Effects of Psilocybin-Assisted Therapy," 487.

18. Gukasyan et al., "Efficacy and Safety," 155–56.

19. Raison et al., "Single-Dose Psilocybin," 843.

Recent studies are showing that ketamine is "a fast-acting—albeit temporary—treatment for depression."[20] Both ketamine and psilocybin are known for rapid effects in reducing depression. Ketamine's effects, however, tend to last for a few days to a few weeks. After that, another treatment session is often needed. The anti-depressant effects of psilocybin, on the other hand, tend to last much longer. For now, however, the advantage of ketamine over psilocybin for the treatment of depression rests in the fact that patients and providers have legal access to ketamine.[21]

Applying psychedelic-assisted therapy to bipolar depression is challenging, although there is some optimism among researchers that it might be effective for bipolar disorder II. Unfortunately, bipolar disorder I depression involves manic episodes that some experts fear could be made worse by psychedelics. As researchers explain, "classic psychedelics seem to be associated with the induction of mania," at least according to "user reports or case studies."[22] In a psychedelic-assisted therapy study of fifteen patients with bipolar II depression, however, researchers reported that "most participants met remission criteria" shortly after the session and "most remained in remission 12 weeks post-dose with no increase in mania/hypomania symptoms or suicidality."[23]

Getting the news that one has cancer can be personally devastating. The effects can include depression, but experts tend to distinguish the more common forms of depression from the sudden distress and anxiety that can be triggered by the onset of a terminal illness. Even before researchers were studying the benefits of psychedelics for depression, some were already beginning to look at whether drugs like psilocybin might help in palliative care by relieving distress.

How one deals with a devastating diagnosis has consequences not just for the treatment process but for interpersonal relationships. For some, the stress and pain caused by such news

20. Mitchell and Anderson, "Psychedelic Therapies Reconsidered," 99.

21. Gukasyan et al., "Efficacy and Safety," 157.

22. Bosch et al., "Psychedelics in the Treatment," 1.

23. Aaronson et al., "Single-Dose Synthetic Psilocybin," 556.

can be overwhelming, bringing on a numbness that is emotionally and spiritually draining. In the context of palliative care, the term "existential distress" is most often used to describe this condition. It is "characterized by hopelessness, loss of meaning and dignity, suicidal ideation, increased pain perception, feeling like a burden to others, and death anxiety."[24] One research team estimates that "anxiety and/or depressive symptoms are common in patients with cancer, present in 30–40% of patients in hospital settings."[25] While depression and anxiety may be the symptoms that stand out, other mental health problems are commonly present, "including medication non-adherence, increased health care utilization, adverse medical outcomes, decreased quality of life, decreased social function, increased disability, hopelessness, increased pain, increased desire for hastened death, increased rates of suicide, and decreased survival rates."[26]

Therapies that involve the use of psilocybin seem to be very promising in trying to help patients suffering from existential distress. One study makes this claim: "Single moderate-dose psilocybin, in conjunction with psychotherapy, produced rapid, robust, and sustained clinical benefits in terms of reduction of anxiety and depression in patients with life threatening cancer."[27] Another report notes that drugs like psilocybin "appear to be well-tolerated and effective in both the short and longer term, with beneficial effects on depression, anxiety, existential distress, and a variety of psychological domains such as quality of life and well-being." Overall, the results "are promising."[28]

A summary of follow-up studies also provides support for the idea of psychedelic-assisted therapy to help those suffering with existential distress. "After 3 years, there were still reductions in anxiety, depression, hopelessness, and demoralization, death anxiety was significantly lower, and spiritual well-being

24. Schimmel et al., "Psychedelics for the Treatment," 15.

25. Ross et al., "Rapid and Sustained," 1165.

26. Ross et al., "Rapid and Sustained," 1165.

27. Ross et al., "Rapid and Sustained," 1175.

28. Schimmel et al., "Psychedelics for the Treatment," 28.

was improved compared to base line. . . . Findings from qualitative studies show that patients also experienced other important outcomes, such as better insights in existing relationships, improved access to one's feelings, increased self-acceptance and -esteem, and acceptance of their illness."[29] Elsewhere we read: "Psilocybin experiences were reported as highly meaningful and spiritual, and associated with positive cognitive, affective, spiritual, and behavioral effects lasting weeks to months."[30]

THE EXPANDING SCOPE OF PSYCHEDELIC THERAPY

Bill Wilson, the founder of Alcoholics Anonymous or AA, was known during his lifetime as Bill W. In the fifties when Bill learned about LSD, he began to wonder whether this new drug would help alcoholics have the sort of spiritual experiences that could help them find recovery. Central to AA and to the wider recovery movement is the idea that at their base, addictions are spiritual problems. In his own recovery, Bill had awakened spiritually only when his alcoholism was about to take his life—too late, in other words, for many alcoholics. What if a spiritual awakening could come earlier?

Through his contacts with the leading LSD researchers of his day, Bill recognized "that LSD could reliably occasion the kind of spiritual awakening he believed one needed in order to get sober." But when he proposed using LSD as part of the work of AA, "his colleagues on the board of the fellowship strongly disagreed, believing that to condone the use of any mind-altering substance risked muddying the organization's brand and message."[31]

What worried Bill's colleagues in AA was that treating one substance addiction by depending on another substance seemed like a dangerously confusing message. As the sixties and seventies

29. Schimmel et al., "Psychedelics for the Treatment," 26.

30. Ross et al., "Rapid and Sustained," 1176.

31. Pollan, *How to Change Your Mind*, 153.

went along, support for their objection only grew. In the meantime, AA continued its work and the recovery movement expanded not just in numbers but in scope, with recovery programs for a wide range of addictions.

Despite the effectiveness of the recovery movement, alcohol abuse continues to claim its victims. According to a recent study, almost seven hundred thousand American adults die per year in ways that were "attributable to excessive alcohol consumption." The study notes that "an estimated 1 in 8 total deaths among US adults aged 20 to 64 years were attributable to excessive alcohol use, including 1 in 5 deaths among adults aged 20 to 49 years."[32] Whether it is through alcohol-related heart disease, cancer, accidental death, or liver disease, the study claims that in the United States, "excessive alcohol use is a leading preventable cause of premature death."[33] In terms of the potential for psychedelic-assisted therapy in treating alcohol abuse disorder, the most promising study so far claims that "psilocybin administered in combination with psychotherapy was associated with robust and sustained decreases in drinking, which were greater than those observed following active placebo with psychotherapy."[34]

Abuse of alcohol, of course, is not the only substance addition that leads to major health problems. Deaths from tobacco are also measured in millions, with about half a million per year in the US alone. According to the World Health Organization, roughly eight million people die of tobacco-related causes each year worldwide, with tobacco killing one half of all users who do not quit. Stopping the use of tobacco, however, is difficult because of the addictive powers of nicotine.

A small pilot study published in 2014 surprised most experts in the field by how promising psilocybin seemed to be as a component of a broader therapy program.[35] In a 2017 follow-up report, the study team interviewed their volunteers again. They found

32. Esser et al., "Estimated Deaths," 6.

33. Esser et al., "Estimated Deaths," 2.

34. Bogenschutz et al., "Percentage of Heavy Drinking Days," 960.

35. Johnson et al., "Pilot Study."

that participants in their study, tested one year and more after the original treatment, were tobacco-free at a level of 60 percent. According to the report, using psilocybin in their treatment protocol meant that they were "approximately doubling the odds of success at initial follow-up."[36]

Reflecting on the study's broader implications, the researchers claimed that their findings show that substances like psilocybin "may hold therapeutic potential in treating a variety of substance use disorders in the context of a structured treatment program. Considering the often chronic and intractable nature of addictive disorders, further investigation of psychedelic-facilitated treatment of addiction and underlying neurobiological mechanisms represent important future directions for research."[37]

Given the high rates of tobacco-related deaths, any program that significantly reduces tobacco use will have profound implications for public health. As a result, Johns Hopkins University was awarded the first National Institutes of Health (NIH) research grant involving psychedelics in fifty years to fund a three-year, multi-site study on the potential benefits of psilocybin on tobacco addiction.

Whether psychedelics may play a role in treating other substance abuse disorders is an open question. Some experts think that drugs like psilocybin may be shown to be widely effective in treating a range of addictions.[38] Early trials are asking whether psilocybin-assisted therapy might be effective in treating substance disorders involving alcohol, tobacco, cocaine, opioids, and methamphetamine.[39] One group of researchers is taking a psychedelic-assisted therapy approach to gambling addiction, expanding the scope of possibilities beyond substance addictions to behavioral addictions.[40]

---

36. Johnson et al., "Long-Term Follow-up," 58.
37. Johnson et al., "Long-Term Follow-up," 58.
38. Brett et al., "Exploring Psilocybin-Assisted Psychotherapy."
39. van der Meer et al., "Therapeutic Effect of Psilocybin in Addiction."
40. Mundall, "Psychedelic Therapy."

Psychedelics are also being proposed as a way to offset at least some of the symptoms of Alzheimer's disease, which is "the most common cause of dementia" and ranks seventh as the "leading cause of death globally . . . reaching a staggering population prevalence above 30% in people over 85."[41] Despite the expenditure of tens of billions of dollars for research, biomedical treatments for Alzheimer's are largely unsuccessful. Some experts, aware that psychedelics can stimulate the growth of new neurons in the human brain, have begun to consider whether these drugs might offer some effective countermeasures to the development of dementia.[42]

Several psychedelics have "rapid plastogenic effects on diverse processes of cognition, learning and memory." It has been shown that their "robust and sustained therapeutic effects involve stimulation of structural and functional dynamics of neuroplasticity, modification of synaptic plasticity, induction of anti-inflammatory effects, and rewiring pathological neurocircuitry," leading to the suggestion that they might be "ideal agents to address neurological, behavioral and psychological features of cortical or subcortical atrophy exhibited in neurodegenerative conditions."[43] Beyond treating those diagnosed with Alzheimer's, it is also being suggested that other problems associated with the aging human brain might be offset at least in part with psychedelics.[44]

Some experts who study psychedelics are asking whether these substances might offer a way to treat autism spectrum disorder (ASD), which affects 1–2 percent of the population. ASD involves problems in social interaction, communication, and attention to others. No treatments are available for addressing the underlying condition. "Instead, antipsychotics, antidepressants, mood stabilizers, and stimulants are used to target ASD-associated features, such as irritability, anxiety, and depression."[45] In light of some of

41. Winkelman et al., "Potential of Psychedelics," 4.

42. Garcia-Romeu et al., "Psychedelics as Novel Therapeutics."

43. Winkelman et al., "Potential of Psychedelics," 6.

44. Winkelman et al., "Potential of Psychedelics," 11.

45. Markopoulos et al., "Evaluating the Potential Use," 2.

the ways in which psychedelics promote social interaction while resolving depression and anxiety, a team of researchers suggests that these substances might "enhance social behaviour and elicit empathogenic effects" while relieving "depression, generalized anxiety, and social anxiety in particular," perhaps in ways that will help those struggling with ASD.[46]

Another mental health disorder that might be alleviated by the use of psychedelics is obsessive-compulsive disorder (OCD). The disorder "is characterized by obsessions (recurrent, intrusive thoughts, images, or impulses that induce significant anxiety or distress) and compulsions (repetitive and/or ritualized physical or mental actions undertaken in an attempt to reduce that anxiety or distress). As OCD progresses, it is often disabling and chronic."[47] One theory about how psychedelics act in the human brain suggests that these drugs loosen prior beliefs, opening the mind to new ideas. If so, then it might make sense to turn to psychedelics for treatment of OCD and other forms of recurring or obsessive thoughts.

PSYCHEDELICS FOR EVERYONE?

The scope of possible mental health applications for psychedelics seems almost unlimited. Some researchers, in fact, are suggesting that we should think of these drugs not as specific treatments for this or that diagnostic category, but as pathways to a more generalized condition of overall mental well-being. Rather than just trying to treat specific disorders, the goal for mental health research would be to find out what makes people healthier overall. Improvements in mental well-being could relieve societies of some of the suffering and costs associated with mental illness. "Mental health problems are currently among the leading causes of disability worldwide, with substantial personal, social, and

---

46. Markopoulos et al., "Evaluating the Potential Use," 2.

47. Ching et al., "Safety, Tolerability," 2.

economic costs attached."[48] If psychedelics contribute to overall mental health, their economic impact would be enormous.

A broadly defined concept like "mental well-being" resonates with traditional philosophical ideas of happiness or *eudaimonia*, which served as the starting point for Aristotle's *Ethics* and has influenced Western thought ever since. Various researchers are beginning to ask whether there is evidence to support the idea that psychedelics can contribute to happiness, although it seems that "contemporary researchers have not reached consensus on what exactly constitutes eudaimonia."[49] A more recent parallel is found in the rise of "positive psychology," which focuses on experiences and traits that contribute to mentally healthy lives. Expanding the circle even further, various disciplines including theology have recently joined public conversations about the meaning of human flourishing, an idea rooted not just in Aristotle but in many philosophical and religious traditions.

General physical health also seems to be improved by the use of psychedelics. The evidence for this does not come from a clinical trial but from an online survey of those who have used psychedelics. The study claimed that those "who reported having ever used a classic psychedelic had significantly higher odds of greater self-reported overall health and significantly lower odds of being overweight or obese." Those who had used psychedelics also reported lower levels of heart disease and cancer. According to the authors of the study, their findings "suggest that lifetime classic psychedelic use is associated with higher odds of better physical health status, which demonstrates the need for more rigorous research to better understand potential causal pathways of classic psychedelics on physical functioning."[50]

All this might leave us wondering whether the claims being made about psychedelic drugs are just so much psychedelic renaissance hype. We can be certain that not every claim for psychedelic-assisted therapy will hold up in future research. But even if only a

48. Mans et al., "Sustained, Multifaceted Improvements," 2.

49. Mans et al., "Sustained, Multifaceted Improvements," 2.

50. Simonsson et al., "Associations between Lifetime," 450.

small part of what is being published by medical researchers leads to safe and effective treatments, we cannot help but wonder how these substances can do all these things. What do we know about how psychedelics act in the human body and brain?

3

The Multiple Levels of Psychedelic Action

EACH HUMAN BEING IS a multi-level system, and psychedelics act at every level. They have profound effects on our consciousness, bringing on subjective states of experience that are meaningful and seem to deepen our connection with other people, the natural world around us, and the transcendent dimensions beyond ordinary reality. At the same time, psychedelics are molecules that act directly on the molecules and cells of our bodies and brains. They change the ways our bodies and brains work. They are present and active in the human system for hours, but they also act in ways that last for months and years.

Compared to most other drugs, psychedelics are odd. They interact with the molecules of the brain in surprising ways, causing a virtual cascade of events, some short-term, some mid-term, and some lasting a lifetime. They act fast, bringing about intense subjective experiences in a matter of minutes or alterations in mood that are felt within hours or days. Their effects, however, tend to last longer than most drugs. Those taking an SSRI generally need to take a tablet every day for the drug to be effective. A single session with psilocybin, on the other hand, can be therapeutic for months or years.

With most drugs, there is no thought to subjective experience. In fact, people often have trouble remembering whether they took their pills. That does not happen with psychedelics. In fact, the subjective experience is so noticeable, so intense, and so disruptive that it creates a serious problem for researchers when they want double blind studies. It also complicates the process of providing psychedelic-assisted therapy. Before, during, and after a session with psychedelics, patients must have support that is likely to be complicated and expensive. The fact that one or two sessions might provide lasting relief could offset some of the costs.

Understanding how psychedelics work at each level of the human system is an intellectual challenge with practical implications. Intellectually, studying the way these drugs work should disabuse us of reductionism or single-level ways of thinking, as if we humans were nothing but our biochemistry or our rationality. Those who use psychedelics tend to shift from reductionism to other, more complex views of the role of mind in nature.

One of the practical implications has to do with the transdiagnostic scope of psychedelic mental health benefits. If psychedelic-assisted therapy moves forward as predicted, mental health therapists working with patients diagnosed with more than one condition might try to leverage the transdiagnostic scope of psychedelics, hoping for a kind of bundling approach to the healing process. Another practical implication of the peculiar features of psychedelics might involve substance abuse disorders when patients are abusing more than one substance, as they often do.[1] Psychedelic-assisted therapy might be a path to a broad or generalized healing process that somehow goes deeper than any single form of addiction. Another practical implication of the odd features of psychedelics adds up to a simple word of caution. Anyone offering these drugs as treatments must be ready to meet their patients at every level, from the most basic physiological needs to their most profound psychological and spiritual transformations.

1. Brett et al., "Exploring Psilocybin-Assisted Psychotherapy."

PSYCHEDELICS IN THE HUMAN BRAIN

When people use psychedelics, the drugs act at the multiple levels of human complexity, from the biochemistry of our brains to the psycho-social networks of our shared humanity. Every level of interaction is important in understanding the full power of psychedelics. At the most basic level of their biochemistry, psychedelics act on brain cells because of their structural similarity to neurotransmitters. This is especially true for the so-called "classic psychedelics" like LSD, psilocybin, DMT, and mescaline. They act by mimicking the brain's own neurotransmitter, serotonin. Psilocybin, for example, metabolizes or converts in the body to psilocin, which has a molecular structure almost identical to serotonin. Psilocin binds to serotonin receptor sites, specifically to the serotonin 2A receptor (5-HT2AR), activating the receiving neuron as if it had just received a "message" from serotonin.

This action in the brain is an essential component of the complex story of psychedelic action. The interplay between classic psychedelics and neurotransmitters is foundational to any explanation of psychedelic action, but it is just a small part of the story. It leaves out complexities at play even at the molecular level, and it is questionable how well it explains the action of drugs other than the classic psychedelics. As one team of experts points out, the "not-so-classic psychedelics" work differently because they "activate serotonin receptors indirectly or not at all." Some of them "work through binding to a combination of receptors (including glutamatergic, dopaminergic, and opioidergic receptors)." But they "would all be considered psychedelic if they demonstrate the capacity for allowing greater access to the psyche in a manner similar to the classic psychedelics."[2] LSD activates dopamine, for example. MDMA acts on the brain's serotonin system when it stimulates the brain to release massive amounts of its own serotonin. This natural serotonin binds to receptors, triggering some of the same subjective effects as psilocybin even though it acts in a different way. Other neurotransmitters are also activated

---

2. Mitchell and Anderson, "Psychedelic Therapies Reconsidered," 96.

by various psychedelics. "Even the classical psychedelics—such as LSD and psilocybin—interact with numerous receptors other than 5-HT2A. Studies differ on which are necessary for the drugs' proposed psychiatric benefits."[3]

What exactly is going on here, even at the molecular level? Experts are not sure, but one thing seems to stand out. Psychedelics act quickly and massively, not just interacting with neurotransmitter systems but flooding them, almost overwhelming them. People involved in trials sometimes speak of waves of empathy. Researchers describe "negative thinking" as being "upended, interrupted, and really blown apart by these psychedelics."[4]

Experts are only beginning to connect the lines of interaction between the molecules of psychedelic agents and brain functions. "The way that ketamine, for instance, might combat symptoms of depression and PTSD is mysterious. The drug binds to and blocks the NMDA receptor, a channel on the surface of neurons that is deeply tied to forming new connections. Blocking it triggers a parade of molecular events that had not previously been linked to depression."[5] In other words, by learning about psychedelics, scientists are also learning new things about the neurology of mental illness.

While psychedelics create plenty of drama at the molecular level, this is only the first or most basic level in the complex, interactive, multi-tiered human system. One surprise from recent research is that psychedelics stimulate the growth of new neurons. The brain naturally produces a signalling molecule called brain-derived neurotrophic factor (BDNF), which stimulates the growth and development of new neurons over the human lifespan. SSRIs like Prozac can bind to BDNF receptors, triggering neuron growth and rewiring. Researchers have now discovered that psychedelics can also bind to BDNF receptors, but with a big difference: "Conventional antidepressants, such as Prozac (fluoxetine), bind to the receptor, too, but the binding is up to 1,000 times stronger for

3. Reardon, "Psychedelic Treatments," 23.

4. Beans, "If Psychedelics Heal," 2.

5. Reardon, "Psychedelic Treatments," 23.

psychedelics. That could explain why these drugs seem to improve symptoms in hours, whereas conventional antidepressants might take months."[6]

When BDNF receptors are stimulated, new neurons are generated, a process that neuroscientists refer to as "neurogenesis." The 1000x power of psychedelics to stimulate neurogenesis has generated a lot of interest in the global research community. It probably helps explain how psychedelics can have such broad, transdiagnostic benefits. It might also show why psychedelics have lasting consequences for the brain. The drugs may leave the brain after a few hours, but the newly produced neurons and their dendritic spines or cell-to-cell connections remain active and functional as an enduring neural legacy.

In addition to creating new neurons, psychedelics also promote what experts call *neuroplasticity* or brain cell reorganization. "According to one definition, neuroplasticity is the ability of the nervous system to reorganize its structure, function, and connections in response to a changing environment or a shifting set of demands, thus constituting the mechanism of neuronal adaptability."[7] Some researchers now refer to psychedelics as *psychoplastogens* because they can reorganize neural networks and modify their functions, thereby "making them promising treatments of neuropsychiatric diseases through regenerating pathological neural circuitry, restoring network-level functioning and enhancing diverse processes."[8] The action of psychedelics on brain networks is the next part of the story of their multi-level effects.

PSYCHEDELICS AND BRAIN NETWORKS

Neurogenesis and neuroplasticity are both natural functions of the brain, two aspects of a broader process that makes new neurons and dendrite connections and weaves them into new neural

6. Reardon, "Psychedelic Treatments," 23.

7. Kočárová et al., "Does Psychedelic Therapy," 7.

8. Winkelman et al., "Potential of Psychedelics," 5.

structures or pathways. Taken together, these processes allow the brain to learn new things and to renew itself, at least up to a point. New brain cells, new connections between them, and renewed neural networks are the result, all part of a dynamic process of "removing and adding new cellular components (neurite branches, synaptic endings) and even cells (nerve cells and associated glial cells) and their connections and structures."[9] New research is showing that psychedelics boost these processes of neurogenesis and neuroplasticity, helping boost the brain's capacity for regrowth and reorganization. With this idea in mind, some have suggested the equivalent of a psychedelic moonshot, hoping that these drugs might slow down or stop dementia.

Using today's advanced brain imaging techniques, researchers are learning how psychedelics desynchronize the rhythmic inter-relationships between various modules across key brain networks. Brain cells are organized in networks that communicate within themselves and with other networks in synchronized waves of electrical energy. One network of special interest among brain scientists is the "default mode network" (DMN). Some experts describe it as the most likely center of self-consciousness in the brain. If the ego has a location, some claim it is in the DMN. One idea is that the DMN is associated with our narrative sense of self. When we are concentrating on a task and not focused on ourselves, the activity of the DMN is reduced. When we are resting or daydreaming, it increases.

Psychedelics change the normal activity of key networks like the DMN. Several studies involving different psychedelics suggest that when the drugs are active in the brain, the DMN becomes less active or communicative within itself and more actively connected with other networks. During this period of a few hours, it could be that the brain's high-level controls are reduced or "relaxed."

A research team led by Robin Carhart-Harris suggests that psychedelics loosen the high-level patterns of beliefs that ordi-narily help us make sense of the world. The idea is that ordinarily, sensory input would overwhelm the brain's ability to make sense of

9. Winkelman et al., "Potential of Psychedelics," 5–6.

what is going on unless the brain can quickly organize perceptions into patterns based on prior experiences. Most of the time, these patterns are helpful, even essential. But they can limit our way of seeing things. Perhaps what psychedelics do is relax the strength of these patterns. The Carhart-Harris team calls their theory "relaxed beliefs under psychedelics" or REBUS. Psychedelics temporarily shake up the brain's normal predictive patterns, "potentially accounting for phenomena such as the dissolution of ego boundaries and potential (long-term) revision of high-level priors, perspectives, or beliefs."[10]

This can be therapeutic, they argue, for people who are trapped in old and self-destructive patterns of thought. Disrupting a person's "hierarchical levels has the most dramatic psychological consequences." Relaxing the hold of old ideas can also lead to new insight, according to the REBUS theory. "This is because the relevant 'aha' or 'eureka' experiences typically emerge spontaneously, 'out of the blue,' as simple, elegant solutions, presumably because redundant models and/or model parameters have been unconsciously stripped away, leaving the 'bare truth beneath.'"[11]

Not everyone studying psychedelics is convinced that the DMN plays such an important role or that the REBUS theory is the final word. Pointing to evidence that psychedelics increase neurogenesis and neuroplasticity, one review team argues that "given the complex multi-modal nature of self-processing, a single neural correlate such as the DMN may not fully capture the complexities of the self-processing concept. . . . Psychedelics alter global brain connectivity, of which the DMN is but one."[12]

Given all the ways that psychedelics interact with the brain's molecules and cells, REBUS may describe just one piece of the action. It does seem true that "psychedelics act as destabilizers, creating the conditions for the dismantling of overly reinforced set points or attractors that underlie symptoms of mental illness." It is as if the brain's structure is disrupted just enough to produce "a

10. Carhart-Harris and Friston, "REBUS and the Anarchic Brain," 321.

11. Carhart-Harris and Friston, "REBUS and the Anarchic Brain," 332.

12. Kelly et al., "Psychedelic Therapy's Transdiagnostic Effects," 16.

topological reconfiguration of the global energy landscape of the mind and brain."[13] Central to REBUS is the idea that psychedelics disrupt or desychronize the rhythmic waves of electrical energy responsible for stability in mental activity. When that happens, entropy or disorder is slightly increased, just enough to loosen things up but not so much that complete disorder takes over. This theory is referred to as "the entropic brain."[14]

Some researchers are asking how psychedelics act elsewhere in the body, perhaps directly on other organs or systemwide. Over the past decades, scientists have learned how the human body and brain interact, sometimes using the same molecules in the brain as in the gut, and sometimes by interacting with the microbiome, the astoundingly complex population of microbes that live within healthy human bodies. Research involving psychedelics, however, is focused almost entirely on brains. A recent paper laments this fact, suggesting that psychedelic scientists are "broadly neglecting the rest of the body." The authors of the paper call attention to the heart, or what they call the "entropic heart," suggesting that the disruptive effects of psychedelics found in brain rhythms might also be found in the rhythmic patterns of the heart.

They point to recent work in cardiology that suggests that the heart does not just beat with monosyllabic regularity, as if it were a mechanical pump. "These empirical findings support the view that the heart is not a mere metronome, but rather a flexible organ that dynamically supports interactions with a complex and changing environment."[15] Researchers are trying to understand how flexibility in the rhythms of the heart can be connected positively to overall health. Psychedelics modify not just the heart rate but also its more subtle patterns, increasing heart rhythm variability or entropy. Ordinarily when the heart rate increases, it is "typically accompanied by decreases in heart variability." Psychedelics, however, increase the rate and the variability or the "entropy" at the same time. Such "simultaneous increases of both

13. Hipólito et al., "Pattern Breaking," 10.
14. Carhart-Harris et al., "Entropic Brain."
15. Rosas et al., "Entropic Heart," 1–2.

have been observed in profiles associated to emotions such as 'joy.'"[16] How does one even begin to connect this with our broader understanding of the biological effects of psychedelics? Is the "entropic heart" a mere "nuisance signal"? Perhaps we should see that "these changes are part of the experience itself, and therefore the corresponding signals may be a bearers [sic] of signal rather than noise."[17]

PSYCHEDELICS AND PSYCHOLOGY

The multiple actions of psychedelics at the cellular level trigger effects felt at the psychological level. Psychedelics act directly on the molecules and cells, but the indirect effects are felt by human beings in the conscious life of subjective awareness, emotion, and personality traits. As they try to understand the full scope of psychedelic action, some scientists describe the effects of psychedelics in the categories of psychology. One obvious reason for doing so has to do with mental health therapy. Mental health disorders like depression and PTSD may be part of common jargon, but they also have precise technical definitions and diagnostic criteria that are described in the *Diagnostic and Statistical Manual of Mental Disorders.*[18] If psychedelics are shown to be effective, the evidence of benefits must align with the criteria for the disorder.

Beyond the technicalities of diagnostic categories, however, various theories and traditions in psychology have played a role in shaping the conversation around psychedelics and their relationship to religious experience. The impact of William James endures in the 2022 publication by David Yaden and Andrew Newberg of *The Varieties of Spiritual Experience,* which updates the work of James by bringing new methods of neuroscience into dialogue with psychology and religious studies.[19] Other formative figures in

---

16. Rosas et al., "Entropic Heart," 5.
17. Rosas et al., "Entropic Heart," 6.
18. American Psychiatric Association, *Diagnostic and Statistical Manual.*
19. Yaden and Newberg, *Varieties.*

psychology, such as Sigmund Freud or Carl Jung, remain influential in today's psychedelics research. For example, some of the original studies of the possible role of the default mode network likened the function of that network to the Freudian ego, which seems to be loosened in its authority when psychedelics are present.[20]

It has also been suggested that psychedelics work in the human system by increasing "psychological flexibility," defined as a capacity for responsiveness and resilience. In more technical terms, psychological flexibility is seen "as a set of psychological processes that help people manage stressors and engage in adaptive behaviors promoting value driven action." Those with psychological flexibility "have the capacity to recognize and adapt to various contextual demands, shift their mindset or behaviors during individual and social experiences, maintain balance across important life domains, and learn to be open to, aware of, and committed to behaviors congruent with their values." Rather than being locked in to one way of thinking, a person with psychological flexibility can consider alternatives or creative possibilities. As a capacity, psychological flexibility is connected directly to well-being.[21] With that definition in mind, researchers make the claim that intense subjective experiences associated with psychedelics are linked with greater psychological flexibility. "Results also showed that the acute psychedelic effects (mystical experience and emotional breakthrough) were associated with greater improvements in psychological flexibility."[22]

A reduced capacity for psychological flexibility seems to "underlie a broad spectrum of psychopathologies. Excessively constrained thought may occur in depression, PTSD/anxiety, OCD, addiction, and eating disorders, whereas excessively variable thought may occur in ADHD or some personality disorders." Some researchers think that increasing psychological flexibility through the use of psychedelics may explain the wide-ranging transdiagnostic scope of these drugs. Psychedelic-enhanced psychological

20. Carhart-Harris et al., "Entropic Brain."
21. Davis et al., "Increases in Psychological Flexibility," 2.
22. Davis et al., "Increases in Psychological Flexibility," 3.

flexibility, in other words, is "a potential transdiagnostic mediator of psychedelic therapy."[23] One group suggests a kind of inverse relationship. If psychedelic-enhanced psychological flexibility has transdiagnostic benefit, it is because its opposite, psychological inflexibility, can be "described as a transdiagnostically relevant pathological phenomenon," basic to a wide range of mental health disorders.[24]

How much flexibility is too much? When does it become a lowering of the usual boundaries that keep us safe from embracing ideas or behaviors that we will later regret? In other words, when does healthy flexibility become risky suggestibility? Those who study psychedelics are aware of the tendency of these drugs to heighten suggestibility when they actively present in the system.[25] Among experts there seems to be general agreement that these drugs enhance the influence of suggestion, worrisome because it means that drug sessions increase the vulnerability of people who might agree to ideas or behaviors that they ordinarily would find wrong or offensive. As a precaution, psychedelic sessions that are part of approved studies have two therapists in the room at all times.

The idea of psychological flexibility is interesting and helpful because it suggests a way to think about the lasting impact of the intense subjective experiences associated with psychedelics. The intense experience lasts for hours or maybe a day or two, but the capacity for psychological flexibility endures for months, maybe for years. "These findings add to a growing literature indicating a central role for acute subjective effects of psychedelics in influencing subsequent mental health outcomes." According to researchers, "psychological flexibility may be an important factor related to those outcomes."[26] This may relate to the belief by many who use psychedelics that the drugs make them more creative.

---

23. Kelly et al., "Psychedelic Therapy's Transdiagnostic Effects," 18.

24. Kočárová et al., "Does Psychedelic Therapy," 4.

25. Carhart-Harris et al., "LSD Enhances Suggestibility."

26. Davis et al., "Increases in Psychological," 7.

It has also been suggested that psilocybin can change the level of the personality trait of "Openness," one of psychology's "big five" traits that tend to be fairly stable over a lifetime. Analyzing data from one psilocybin trial, researchers "observed significant increases in Openness after a high-dose psilocybin session that were larger in magnitude than changes in personality typically observed in healthy adults over decades of life experience."[27] They found that an intense mystical or spiritual experience during the psychedelic session played a key role in whether the change in personality was lasting. They found a link between the level of mystical experience reported by participants and the level of "enduring increases in Openness, suggesting that other mystical experiences could occasion similar change." They added that the connection between intense experience and lasting change was consistent with other findings from other studies. "Qualitative research has documented sudden and dramatic positive changes in attitudes, values, and behaviors following spontaneous mystical or spiritual experiences."[28]

The connection between psychedelics and subjective experiences will be explored more fully in the final section of this chapter. First, however, it is important to consider how psychedelics sometimes lead to difficult or challenging experiences.

CHALLENGING EXPERIENCES

Psychedelics interact with human bodies and brains in many ways, sometimes disrupting or interfering with the ordinary functions of neurotransmitters, brain cells, neural networks, or other organs throughout the body. These disruptions can bring healing, but they can also be confusing, distressing, even nightmarish. Once called "bad trips," disturbing psychedelic experiences are now called "challenging" or "difficult."

---

27. MacLean et al., "Mystical Experiences Occasioned," 1457.
28. MacLean et al., "Mystical Experiences Occasioned," 1460.

In clinical trials, challenging psychedelic experiences are considered rare. Most researchers recognize that they do happen, that they present a significant concern that must be addressed, and that there is nothing to be gained by ignoring them or minimizing their significance. At the same time, most would see them as manageable when the right precautions are in place. For example, research volunteers must be carefully screened for overall health, and those with mental health conditions like schizophrenia or bipolar disorder are currently excluded.

The use of psychedelics outside clinical settings is another matter, especially in view of the wide-ranging contexts in which people use these drugs, from underground sessions with experienced guides to festivals and raves. Online surveys can gather useful information, but their reliability when it comes to the prevalence of challenging experiences is questionable. "The prevalence of challenging, difficult, or distressing experiences using classic psychedelics has not yet been examined in nationally representative samples free of significant self-selection bias, but the frequency and intensity of such experiences appear to be higher in naturalistic surveys than in laboratory studies."[29] One research group summarized results of a study involving over 600 respondents. "Notably, 2.6% reported seeking medical, psychiatric, or psychological assistance in the days or weeks following their most challenging, difficult, or distressing experience."[30] Challenging psychedelic experiences are common enough to make them a significant issue. More information is needed to guide policymakers who are thinking of changes in drug laws.

Calling a drug session "challenging" is a highly subjective judgment. "Whether a phenomenon is experienced as 'bad' or 'part of the process' depends on a person's appraisal." Any form of meditation or intense personal experience can have features that are unsettling. Not only might different people use different labels, but individuals might change their assessments over time. "Indeed, the same person might appraise such phenomena differently

29. Simonsson et al., "Prevalence and Associations," 106.
30. Simonsson et al., "Prevalence and Associations," 108.

at different life stages. Some individuals might intentionally use psychedelics as a tool to revisit traumatic memories, while others in our survey reported feeling overwhelmed by the resurfacing of traumatic experiences."[31]

In order to study the problem in a systematic way, one team has developed and tested the "Challenging Experience Questionnaire" (CEQ). It is organized around seven factors: grief, fear, death, insanity, isolation, physical distress, and paranoia. Together, these seven factors "provide a phenomenological profile of challenging aspects of experiences with psilocybin."[32] These seven states of mind, often encountered in combination with each other, can be truly frightening for anyone who experiences them. In clinical settings, skilled therapists are present throughout the drug session, providing immediate comfort and reassurance. Most people using psychedelics, however, are taking them outside of clinical trials. Sometimes they are assisted by a skilled or trained guide, but often they are alone or with a friend.

Surveys also help us understand what people did or failed to do that they think contributed to the difficulties in their experience. One study analyzed responses, listing the five most common factors as "no preparation, negative mindset, no psychological support, disagreeable social environment, and disagreeable physical environment." The report continued by reporting on what was most helpful in dealing with the difficulties. Participants responded by pointing to things like "trying to calm the mind, changing location, asking for help from friend, changing social environment, and smoking cannabis."[33]

Sometimes a difficult experience can turn out to be helpful. What seems painful or distressing at one moment can be seen later as a necessary pathway to deeper insight. This idea of growth through struggle and pain is deeply rooted in religion, myth, and popular culture. It can be a source of hope for anyone experiencing difficult times. It may also place a burden on people to get over

31. Evans et al., "Extended Difficulties," 18.

32. Barrett et al., "Challenging Experience Questionnaire," 1279.

33. Simonsson et al., "Prevalence and Associations," 107.

their fear or grief, to suppress their feelings, or to pretend that they are doing better than they really are, all out of a sense of social expectation. It may be true that "by constructing a narrative which makes sense of challenging experiences, the accompanying emotions tend to resolve more quickly, and the experience takes on a sense of meaning."[34] But is it entirely honest? And if it does not work out that way, does it leave people with enduring psychological trauma, spiritual distress, or self-blame?

THE ROLE OF SUBJECTIVE EXPERIENCES

Subjective experiences associated with psychedelics are often described as deeply meaningful, psychologically enlightening, and spiritually enriching. The spiritual significance of these experiences is the overall theme of this book. Here in this section, however, we are focusing on the question of the role of these experiences in mental health.

There is no question of a correlation between subjective intensity and mental health benefits. There are real questions, however, about how to define these experiences and what role they might play in the healing process. Are subjective experiences necessary for healing? If not, could we develop modified psychedelics that heal without the trip? If on the other hand it turns out that subjective experiences really are necessary for healing, must they be spiritual or mystical in their significance? Or will a generalized subjective intensity do just as well?

The idea that subjective experiences of a spiritual nature make an important difference in the healing process was suggested in a 2014 pilot study of psilocybin as a treatment for tobacco addiction.[35] A few years after the first report was published, researchers went back to their volunteers for a follow-up study. Their report uses the word "spiritual" repeatedly. The authors say that the use of the word was not prompted by how they asked the questions

34. Frymann et al., "The Psychedelic Integration Scales," 5.

35. Johnson et al., "Pilot Study."

but came up spontaneously from the volunteers. "While the intervention used in this study was not explicitly 'spiritual' in nature, participants consistently attributed a high degree of spiritual significance to their psilocybin session experiences, raising questions about the role of spirituality in smoking cessation."[36]

What is most striking in this study is not just the connection between spiritual experience and smoking cessation, but that the level of spiritual or mystical intensity correlates with the level of quitting. This correlation is consistent with other studies. "Several studies suggest that increased levels of spirituality are associated with improved treatment outcomes in substance dependence recovery."[37] Other teams of psychedelic researchers make the same connection. "There exists a large body of evidence to support the principle that the quality of an individual's acute experience under a psychedelic reliably predicts and mediates longer-term psychological outcomes—including changes in mental health outcomes."[38]

Some scientists, however, are cautious when words like "spiritual" start to appear in peer-reviewed scientific journals. If intense subjective experiences are necessary, must they be called mystical or spiritual? "Perspectives differ on how best to refer to intense subjective experiences under psychedelics. Some prefer the more secular term 'peak experience' while the term 'mystical-type experience'…is preferred by others."[39]

Does it really matter what we call it? It obviously does to some of the scientists. Their concern may be mainly methodological. Some of them are quick to point out that science has no business studying mystical or spiritual questions. It is simply not qualified to do so, and they worry that scientific rigor is being compromised. For example, we read that "in light of the encroachment of supernatural and nonempirical beliefs on psychedelic science, we identify shortcomings of this link between mysticism and

36. Johnson et al., "Long-Term Follow-up," 59.
37. Johnson et al., "Long-Term Follow-up," 59.
38. Kočárová et al., "Does Psychedelic Therapy," 7.
39. Kočárová et al., "Does Psychedelic Therapy," 7.

psychedelic research, and we contend that the mysticism framework, along with its associated theories and terminology, should be actively superseded."[40]

For some, however, the objection seems based on more than methodological boundaries. Their resistance to terms like spirituality and mysticism in scientific contexts seems to be rooted in a philosophical or ontological commitment to naturalistic materialism in one form or another. In other words, science should avoid a spiritual dimension, not just because it lacks competence, but because the spiritual dimension is a delusion that science rejects. One team suggests that "a progressive step toward framework agnosticism might be to focus on the mechanisms underlying such experiences."[41] It seems fair to ask whether the use of the word "mechanism" is consistent with "framework agnosticism" or whether it reveals an implicit mechanistic viewpoint.

When properly drawn, methodological boundaries are important and should be respected. It is helpful to ask whether the "use of the mysticism framework creates a 'black box' mentality in which researchers are content to treat certain aspects of the psychedelic state as beyond the scope of scientific inquiry."[42] This is reminiscent of explanations used in the era of early modern science. What could not be explained scientifically was sometimes explained theologically as God's action, important to the outcome but independent of natural causes. This strategy gave rise to a "god of the gaps" mentality that was eventually rejected by scientists and theologians alike. Calling certain experiences mystical or spiritual could amount to the same thing, saying in effect that the mystical is necessary to account for the effect but it is completely off limits for scientific understanding. While scientists are not able to know what people mean when they call their experience mystical or spiritual, that people say they have these experiences is a simple fact. Science can describe how often people say they have these experiences, under what conditions, and what their consequences

40. Sanders and Zijlmans, "Moving Past Mysticism," 1253.

41. Kočárová et al., "Does Psychedelic Therapy," 7.

42. Sanders and Zijlmans, "Moving Past Mysticism," 1253.

might be. Labelling them spiritual does not mean that they cannot be studied scientifically. It only means that some people describe them as such. Whether their reasons for doing so take them beyond science is no concern for science.

The debate over psychedelic subjective experience and whether it should be called "spiritual" is reflective of other debates about human health. "Already, there is a broad movement in medical ethics critiquing bioreductive approaches to treatment, where mental health is conceived of in terms of brain states or chemical processes alone rather than (also) in terms of a person's lived experiences in sociorelational context, and the meanings they give to those experiences as part of a life narrative." Deeper still is the question of what it means to be human: "To be a person, much less a person in good mental health, is to experience and interpret the world in a certain way (or range of ways); it is not simply to be a bearer of nonpathological brain states."[43]

If there is a cultural shift underway today toward greater acceptance of the role that people assign to spirituality in health, there also seems to be a shift of a different sort that is moving us away from religious structures and theological dogmas and toward a more generalized spirituality. Growing discomfort with religion is offset by a growing acceptance of the idea that being spiritual is a healthy and normal part of human flourishing. Not everyone is convinced that spirituality is a good thing or that it can be set free from everything that makes religion objectionable, but movement in this direction seems to be happening.

In the future, some of the patients who seek psychedelic-assisted therapies may worry that drugs will make them spiritual in order to make them healthy. Once treated, they may look back on their experience and agree that this is indeed what has happened. Looking back, they may gladly accept the label of "spiritual" as an appropriate description of their new take on life. Clinical evidence so far suggests that this will happen. "Patients who are treated with psychedelic-assisted therapy often attribute the amelioration of their symptoms to a psychological breakthrough achieved during

43. Yaden et al., "Ethical Issues," 467.

a psychedelic induced altered state of consciousness. This is not surprising given that many people rate psychedelic experiences as being among the most profound and meaningful events in their lives that can lead to long-lasting changes in their worldviews."[44]

It is entirely possible, however, that some candidates for psychedelic-assisted therapy will stay away if they think it has religious overtones. Some might give it a try and find that their mental health has improved but their sense of spirituality is unchanged. One study comments that "many patients treated with psychedelics who do not have full mystical experiences still find psychedelic treatment to be beneficial, while others who do have full mystical experiences do not necessarily experience substantial reduction in disease symptoms."[45]

As research into psychedelic-assisted therapy moves along, it will be important to make these treatments both financially affordable and spiritually accessible to as many people as possible, regardless of their objections to religion or spirituality. If the cost of treatment is a real concern, so is spiritual apprehensiveness. If psychedelic-assisted therapy is approved as part of a therapeutic protocol that includes one or more drug sessions that typically involve intense subjective experiences, these experiences should be offered in ways that are spiritually neutral, at least as far as possible. For this reason alone, informed consent documents will be difficult to create.

The most obvious way to eliminate all the overtones of spirituality from psychedelic-assisted therapy is to get rid of the intense subjective experiences altogether. Some scientists want to do this. Their first question is whether these intense experiences are really necessary for healing. If they are not, then their second question is whether an effective alternative to traditional psychedelics can be created. Using what we know about how psychedelics act on molecules and cells, can we create new drugs that can do the healing work of neurogenesis and neuroplasticity? According to one team of investigators, "if enhanced neural plasticity in key

44. Olson, "Subjective Effects," 564.
45. Olson, "Subjective Effects," 564.

circuits is driving psychedelic-induced changes in behavior, peak mystical experiences may not be necessary for these drugs to treat mental illness."[46]

Whether it is possible for psychedelic-assisted therapy to be effective without the subjective experience is an unsettled scientific question. If it is possible, should it be offered? One argument for doing so is that for some patients, undergoing an intense subjective experience could pose a problem. For example, "the subjective effects of psychedelics could be harmful to some people . . . [and] the subjective effects of psychedelics is indeed contraindicated."[47]

Another advantage of eliminating the need for the subjective experiences is that "the cost of treatment could be reduced as there might be less of a need for active clinical support during the experience of acute subjective effects."[48] If the psychologically intense subjective experiences can be eliminated, mental health treatments would be simpler and cheaper to offer. In all likelihood, that would benefit any pharmaceutical companies that offer such experience-free psychedelic drugs. It would also benefit patients whose access to mental health treatment is currently inadequate. Adding standard psychedelics to mental health therapy will only increase its cost and impede access. Replacing traditional mental health therapy even in part with an occasional pill could reduce costs and expand access, at least in theory.

On the other hand, if it is true that the quality of subjective experience predicts the effectiveness of the treatment, and if the highest quality experience includes a spiritual dimension, then it makes sense that people have the most beneficial subjective experience possible. That requires professional care that is prepared to support patients who want to get the most out of their spiritual experiences. A research group that includes medical chaplains is calling for specialized training for chaplains as spiritual guides that will be available on a strictly optional basis as a standard feature for psychedelic-assisted therapy. If spiritual experiences contribute

46. Olson, "Subjective Effects," 564.

47. Yaden et al., "Ethical Issues," 465.

48. Yaden et al., "Ethical Issues," 465.

to therapy, then these experiences should be a part of the therapy process "in a systematized, nonsectarian (i.e., pluralistic), and scalable way, as is appropriate for any treatment mediator in evidence-based psychotherapy."[49] In addition, they argue that it is important that "other professionals are not neglecting the spiritual, existential, religious, and theological concerns that arise in the course of treatment."[50]

Whether or not this proposal is turned into policy, it is clear that psychedelics are powerful substances that may have great potential for healing but must be handled with care and respect. They act in surprising ways that are not always predictable or easily manageable. People who undergo psychedelic sessions deserve the kind of support that requires careful preparation, professional collaboration, and skill in knowing how to respond when experiences are challenging. Above all, they deserve support when their psychedelic experiences raise questions that invite them to journey into new dimensions of spiritual awareness and growth.

49. Palitsky et al., "Importance of Integrating," 745.
50. Peacock et al., "Spiritual Health," 19.

4

Psychedelics and Spiritual Experiences

WHAT CAN SCIENCE TELL us about psychedelics and spiritual experience? The answer depends at least in part on how scientific researchers define spiritual experience, a question that we will explore in the first section of this chapter. Then we look at how scientists themselves are thinking about the claim made so often by participants in their studies that psychedelic experiences are highly meaningful.

One of the surprising findings from studies into psychedelic spiritual experiences is that people often claim that their experiences changed their views about the nature of reality. Quite simply, it seems that psychedelics can change metaphysical and religious beliefs. We read, for example, that the "percentage of the group that identified as being atheist or agnostic before the encounter (55%) dropped significantly (to 26%) after the encounter, whereas identification of belief in ultimate reality, higher power, God, or universal divinity increased significantly from 36% to 58%."[1]

In the popular press, results like this are sometimes translated badly into headlines that imply that psychedelics can cure atheism. More careful interpretations point to some of the complications

1. Davis et al., "Survey of Entity Encounter Experiences," 1017.

and nuances in what scientists are reporting. At the same time, it seems ironic to many people that scientists are discovering that drugs undermine confidence in the worldview of materialistic scientism. "Many of the metaphysical conclusions that people draw from their psychedelic experiences seem to reach beyond, or be at odds with, what our common experience or our best science allows us to reasonably believe."[2] What should we make of this? Should people be warned that their old beliefs might be threatened? Should those seeking a spiritual awakening be encouraged to use psychedelics as their pathway?

In this chapter we will look more deeply into what science can tell us about spiritual experience. Some of what we learn has obvious theological significance, but the theological implications are taken up later in the final three chapters of the book. It is important to recognize the limits of what science can tell us about spiritual experience. For example, it cannot answer metaphysical or theological questions about the objective correlates of experience. It can, however, tell us how many people claim to have spiritual experiences, how often they occur, and what are some of their most common features. It can also tell us about correlations between spiritual experience and mental health, or whether people who avoid religious affiliation claim to have such experiences.

DEFINING AND MEASURING SPIRITUAL EXPERIENCES

Evidence suggests that spiritual experiences occur frequently. Some speculate that our human ancestors may have had such experiences well before the dawn of recorded history. Several paleontologists think that beginning roughly forty thousand years ago, spiritual experiences played a role in the creation of cave art.

This suggests that spiritual experiences have long been available as a possible subject of scientific study. The idea of studying them scientifically, however, is relatively new. William James

2. Gładziejewski, "From Altered States," 2.

is often seen as the first to explore the field with scientific rigor, most notably in his Gifford Lectures published as *The Varieties of Religious Experience: A Study in Human Nature.*[3] Building on the work of James, the best recent summary of the science of spiritual experiences is *The Varieties of Spiritual Experience* by David Yaden and Andrew Newberg. Yaden and Newberg draw on the tradition of research established by William James, adding their own scientific work as well as research by other scientists, including studies involving psychedelics.

The first step in trying to study spiritual experiences is to define them. "Spiritual experiences," they say, are "mental states."[4] That is not to suggest that spiritual experiences are thoughts or abstract concepts that lack the full emotional and embodied dimensions of human beings. These experiences are emotional and cognitive at once. On the one hand, they "are not merely emotions. They may involve emotions, and emotions often follow, but the experience itself cannot be described only in emotional terms." At the same time, they "also involve cognitive processes and can frequently alter thoughts or beliefs after the fact."[5]

What sets "spiritual experiences" apart from other experiences? The answer comes down to whether the people who have the experiences see them as spiritual. With that simple criterion in place, Yaden and Newberg point to evidence that suggests that spiritual experiences are "surprisingly prevalent," probably involving about 35 percent of the population.[6] At the same time, they note that spiritual experiences are widely varied. They point to the use of the word "varieties" in the title of William James' book, a word they keep in the title of their own book. People who say they have spiritual experiences are not alike, and neither are their experiences. Differences in personality, location, and culture all contribute to the wide range of the ways in which people describe their experiences.

3. James, *Varieties of Religious Experience.*
4. Yaden and Newberg, *Varieties*, 146.
5. Yaden and Newberg, *Varieties*, 146.
6. Yaden and Newberg, *Varieties*, 68–69.

With so much variety, the challenge then is to find the common features. Yaden and Newberg asked people to describe their experiences, and what they found most often is that people say their spiritual experiences tend to point beyond ordinary reality, as if the person having the experience senses or feels that there is some sort of objective referent, even if it is one they cannot describe. Spiritual experiences "include some content having to do with some aspect of reality beyond appearances. That is, one feels as if he or she has contacted something deeper than everyday life." That feeling of something deeper is what sets spiritual experiences apart from other experiences. "Most often, this involves some kind of mind—a god, gods, or other supernatural entities—but it can also involve a perception of an underlying oneness or even beauty in existence. . . . Spiritual experiences typically involve deep feelings of connectedness to the unseen order that is perceived."[7] Yaden and Newberg are clear in their belief that science cannot tell us whether any gods exist, but it can tell us that many people have experiences in which they sense the presence of transcendent dimensions.

Based on their work, Yaden and Newberg reject the idea that spiritual experiences are too diverse to be defined and studied. They reject "the extremes of complete similarity and complete difference," looking instead for a scientifically manageable number of "broad categories" to organize their work. Their categories originate from a process of interviews and questionnaires from which they tease out common themes, which are then clustered and organized according to their importance in the vast database of participant responses. That process, called "factor analysis," led them to group the most important themes around three factors: "Numinous Experiences (involving the presence of God), Mystical Experiences (involving feelings of unity), and Paranormal Experiences (involving the presence of deceased relatives or other nonphysical beings)."[8]

7. Yaden and Newberg, *Varieties*, 146–47.

8. Yaden and Newberg, *Varieties*, 159.

Of the three factors, the numinous stands out as the most highly rated and the most important. "Numinous experience, the feeling of being in touch with divinity or God, may constitute the prototypical religious or spiritual experience." They continue: "Numinous experiences, involving the presence of God or divinity, are among the most prevalent and impactful spiritual experiences."[9] Somewhat like the flip side of numinous experience is the "experience of self-loss." The sense of the presence of something like "God" is mirrored by an awareness that the self is somehow less important than before. If there is a link between the sense of the numinous and the sense of self-loss, Yaden and Newberg suggest it might rest in a feeling of connectedness. They write that "we noticed two components of self-transcendent experiences that seem like logical corollaries, but which can be conceptually differentiated: self-loss and connectedness."[10] They add the "self-loss" or "ego dissolution" is a common feature of spiritual experience, quoting Jonathan Haidt's remark that spiritual experience "is an 'off' button for the self."[11]

It is important to note here that Yaden and Newberg call attention to an important difference between spiritual self-loss and pathological depersonalization, which is "related to another condition in dissociative disorder called derealization, in which the external world feels unreal. Dissociative disorders are a serious form of mental illness," they note, reminding us of the proximity and yet the profound difference between spiritually grounded mental health and mental illness.

Looking back to the work of William James, Yaden and Newberg note that their empirical work confirms the importance of the "noetic quality" as an identifying feature of what James called mystical experiences. James writes: "Although so similar to states of feeling, mystical states seem to those who experience them to be also states of knowledge. They are states of insight into depths of truth unplumbed by the discursive intellect. They are

9. Yaden and Newberg, *Varieties*, 182.

10. Yaden and Newberg, *Varieties*, 233.

11. Yaden and Newberg, *Varieties*, 236.

illuminations, revelations, full of significance and importance, all inarticulate though they remain; and as a rule they carry with them a curious sense of authority."[12] Michael Pollan defines the feeling of the noetic quality this way: "People feel they have been let in on a deep secret of the universe, and they cannot be shaken from that conviction."[13]

The noetic quality is a feeling of the reality or authority being conveyed by the experience. Sometimes that happens when we are dreaming and everything seems real. When we wake up, however, we are usually quick to realize that it was just a dream. "But with spiritual experiences, the experience not only feels real during the experience but also continues to feel real after the spiritual experience is over. This seems to be a unique feature of spiritual experiences, as most of the time we immediately deem intensely altered states of consciousness as less real as soon as we leave them, as in waking from dreams. But the realness of spiritual experiences seems to transcend other epistemic states, including that of everyday reality."[14]

The concept of mystical experience was defined further by W. T. Stace. In his *Mysticism and Philosophy* in 1960, Stace offered his own list of the features of mysticism, derived from but expanded through his own research. In 1962, when Walter Pahnke conducted his famous "Marsh Chapel" or "Good Friday Experiment," he drew directly on Stace to create a questionnaire. Pahnke's questionnaire has been modified over the years, but its categories drawn from Stace remain the most commonly used in the study of mystical or spiritual experiences in the context of psychedelic research. The result is the Mystical Experience Questionnaire, now commonly known as the MEQ. Because of the wide use of the MEQ, "mystical experiences are among the most well-studied kind of spiritual experience."[15] Relying on the MEQ, psychedelic researchers have established the relationship between drugs like psilocybin and

---

12. James, *Varieties of Religious Experience*, 210.

13. Pollan, *How to Change*, 41.

14. Yaden and Newberg, *Varieties*, 296.

15. Yaden and Newberg, *Varieties*, 224.

"mystical experience." They have also shown that high scores on the MEQ are associated with mental health benefits.[16]

In chapter 5, we will see how scholars in religion and theology criticize the work of Stace. Religion scholars object to Stace's perennialism, the notion that there are universal features of mystical experience that transcend cultures. Experts in Christian mysticism believe that Stace fails to represent the core themes of that tradition. Some scientists also express concerns, not so much about Stace in particular but about the use of concepts like the mystical. They are more than a little queasy about mysticism, claiming that it is hopelessly entangled in religion.

Yaden and Newberg are cautious about these studies. They wonder whether it is really a good thing that research using the MEQ "brings the study of spiritual experience to center stage in the study of psychedelics in general."[17] They agree that its use might unlock an entirely new approach to mental health. They note, however, "the term 'mystical experience' tends to have an explicitly religious connotation to many (despite its definition in the scholarly literature as referring to feelings of unity rather than beliefs), which can cause problems when people have them who do not have religious or spiritual beliefs." Later they add this: "As psychedelics enter mainstream research and application in secular healthcare settings, metaphysically loaded, supernatural framings of the topic will likely become increasingly problematic. Indeed, in such healthcare settings we must inevitably strive to demystify the mystical and secularize the spiritual.[18]

While it may not be possible or helpful to "demystify the mystical," their point about religious themes in healthcare settings is entirely valid. Medical institutions in a pluralistic society should be neutral and accommodating of all religions and outlooks on life, and treatment should not have a built-in religious bias. While remaining free of bias for or against any religion, they also need to provide support for clients who express the need to think about

16. Yaden and Newberg, *Varieties*, 230.

17. Yaden and Newberg, *Varieties*, 356.

18. Yaden and Newberg, *Varieties*, 399.

religious ideas as part of the process of therapy. Whether that will be possible for psychedelic-assisted therapy is an open question.[19]

Despite our misgivings about the use of the MEQ to measure "mysticism," researchers have in fact used it to provide critically important scientific support for the claim that psychedelics bring about mystical experiences that are meaningful, enduring, and beneficial for mental health. In what many see as the start of a new era of the scientific study of psychedelic spirituality, the landmark 2006 study makes this claim: "In conclusion, the present study showed that, when administered to volunteers under supportive conditions, psilocybin occasioned experiences similar to spontaneously occurring mystical experiences and which were evaluated by volunteers as having substantial and sustained personal meaning and spiritual significance."[20] This finding was based on the use of the MEQ. Whatever the flaws in Stace or the limits in the MEQ, its use has revolutionized the study of psychedelics and spiritual experience.[21]

THE MEANINGFULNESS OF PSYCHEDELIC SPIRITUAL EXPERIENCES

The 2006 publication not only linked psilocybin with mystical experiences. It also said that research volunteers found their experiences to be surprisingly "meaningful." The original report puts it this way: "It is remarkable that 67% of the volunteers rated the experience with psilocybin to be either the single most meaningful experience of his or her life or among the top five most meaningful experiences of his or her life."[22] Again and again, subsequent studies point to the meaningfulness of psychedelic experiences. What are we to make of the fact that research participants agree that their

19. Palitsky et al., "Importance of Integrating."

20. Griffiths et al., "Psilocybin Can Occasion," 283.

21. Cole-Turner, "Psychedelic Mysticism."

22. Griffiths et al., "Psilocybin Can Occasion," 276.

psychedelic experiences were deeply or profoundly meaningful, the top-level experiences of their lifetime?

The first question, of course, has to do with the meaning of "meaning." Is there a scientific definition or theory of meaningfulness? "The relationship between meaning and psychedelics is everywhere implied; however, we do not currently have any rigorous analyses of this relationship, perhaps due to the lack of a precise definition of meaning."[23] Although they use the concept constantly, the leading experts in the field seem to have no definition of "meaningful" and no causal explanation for the felt meaningfulness of psychedelic experiences. "The same goes for some of the best minds in psychedelic research, who consistently report that psychedelics enhance a subjective sense of meaning without an explicit theory of meaning."[24] According to Ido Hartogsohn, it is Aldous Huxley who offers the most poetic description of meaningfulness. Hartogsohn quotes Huxley's comment that while he is under the influence of mescalin, ordinary objects around him were "all but quivering under the pressure of significance by which they were charged."[25] Then Hartogsohn adds his own description of meaningfulness when he writes that "psychedelics intensify mental phenomena and cause them and their significance to appear bigger, vaster, and more dramatic than otherwise."[26]

The meaningfulness boost that comes from psychedelics seems to be the direct opposite of the effect of SSRIs like Prozac, which are commonly used to treat depression and anxiety. As Hartogsohn points out, SSRIs "diminish the intensity of experience, thereby allowing individuals who are otherwise overwhelmed by feelings to adequately cope and function." After all, it seems reasonable that if someone is anxious about what is going on around them, the best thing to do is to give them something that decreases the meaningfulness of the sources of anxiety. The result is "a less dramatic, more flattened experience of the world. Psychedelics,

23. Plesa and Petranker, "Psychedelics and Neonihilism," 2.
24. Plesa and Petranker, "Psychedelics and Neonihilism," 5.
25. Huxley, *Doors of Perception*, 6.
26. Hartogsohn, "Meaning-Enhancing," 2.

by contrast, are regularly described in these and other accounts as doing the exact opposite: as drugs which amplify consciousness, and augment the intensity of perception, emotional reactions, and neurological indicators such as amygdala response." On the question of "meaningfulness," it seems that SSRIs and psychedelics stand in stark contrast to each other. SSRIs work by "diminishing emotional volume, thereby making experiences more bearable, while psychedelic therapy functions by amplifying emotional volume and demanding that patients 'face the demon.'"[27]

We can try to make sense of meaningfulness by recalling what William James says about the noetic quality of mystical experiences. Drawing on James, Hartogsohn suggests a connection between meaningfulness and the noetic quality as a feeling of truth. A spiritual experience is meaningful because it involves an "experience of gaining access to a profounder, more significant plane of existence imbued with paramount authority and significance which transcend ordinary reality." These themes are connected by scholars after James, such as Rudolf Otto. Religious encounters have a level of intensity that Otto encapsulates in his idea of the numinous or the *mysterium tremendum*. Hartogsohn adds that the "experience of confronting an overwhelming, ineffable, and even unfathomable quality of the world is arguably facilitated by the tendency of psychedelics to imbue the mind and the external world with vibrant significance, as noted by Huxley."[28]

For some today, life itself does not seem to be meaningful. Nothing has any particular significance or self-transcendent value. Whether driven by boredom or fear of emptiness, we pursue what we hope are meaningful experiences, sometimes at great effort or risk or expense. Like it or not, the use of psychedelics and their connection to meaningfulness is embedded within a culture that fears the loss of meaning. According to Hartogsohn, "From a wider theoretical perspective, psychedelics' function as enhancers of meaning can be seen in the broader cultural context of late modernity's struggle to make sense and meaning of life in

27. Hartogsohn, "Meaning-Enhancing," 2.
28. Hartogsohn, "Meaning-Enhancing," 3.

increasingly atomized, individualized, and stress-ridden societies; a difficulty compounded by the disappearing role of religion and the implosion of linear narratives of progress."[29] Mental illness is sometimes connected to this crisis of meaning, especially the "rising prevalence of depression, suicidality, and other psychopathologies in modern societies."[30]

These themes are picked up and explored further by Patric Plesa and Rotem Petranker, who also call attention to the contrast between the meaningfulness associated with psychedelic spiritual experiences and the lack of meaning that is a common theme in our wider cultural context.[31] It is as if psychedelic drugs were being used to create an island of significance and attentiveness in an otherwise flat sea where nothing is worth a second thought, much less a serious commitment. For Plesa and Petranker, the juxtaposition between the meaningful experience and the meaningless culture presents psychedelic mental health researchers with a special challenge. They try to describe the problem by returning to the language of "set and setting," jargon that is familiar to all in psychedelic circles to refer to what the patient brings to the session (set) and what surrounds the patient in the session (setting). The usual "set and setting" does not go far enough because it only focuses on individuals or small groups and leaves out the wider culture.

In order to speak of this wider cultural context, Plesa and Petranker use the term "matrix." If we really want to achieve the greatest therapeutic benefit from psychedelics, we must expand our thinking until it includes set, setting, and matrix. The matrix includes "the social context, including our friends, family members, and work environment, as well as values, beliefs, and attitudes." Viewed this way, we can see how "our cultural values, mores, and norms shape this matrix and the ways in which psychedelics may affect us." The governing assumptions of our culture, they insist, are "individuality, self-sufficiency, and materialism."[32]

---

29. Hartogsohn, "Meaning-Enhancing," 3.

30. Hartogsohn, "Meaning-Enhancing," 3.

31. Plesa and Petranker, "Psychedelics and Neonihilism."

32. Plesa and Petranker, "Psychedelics and Neonihilism," 5.

They refer to this as the "neoliberal social matrix," claiming that it "is related to feelings of alienation, and a lack of clarity regarding what matters in life. It is hostile to the very idea of meaningfulness. Even if psychedelic-assisted therapy is highly successful in treating a range of mental health problems with a drug experience that is "meaningful," in the end just sending patients home "to a matrix of a meaning crisis is a temporary solution at best."[33]

At the very least, researchers need to recognize the problem as a limitation on the effectiveness of therapy. Plesa and Petranker do not assume that psychedelic-assisted therapy can undo the stranglehold of the wider culture. Despite our best efforts, it is probably going to remain true that even if patients feel "a greater sense of connection to their self, their community, or the world, they will still return to a neoliberal culture which enshrines individualization, responsibilization, competition, and self-governance." For the client, it means living in two contradictory cultural spaces at once. After treatment, they "return to their communities with the impossible task of communicating an ineffable experience and its effects on them to their families and friends or, alternatively, processing the experience alone." Failing to describe their experience, "which is inexplicable to one's social circle, may even serve to distance one from their community."[34]

We return to this theme later in the book when we ask whether faith communities may have a role to play in offering what amount to countercultural communities of support, not just for those who are trying to make sense of a meaningful psychedelic experience but for anyone who finds that the culture that surrounds them suffocates them in their search for a spiritual form of life.

PSYCHEDELICS ALTER METAPHYSICAL BELIEFS

Many people hold basic beliefs about the nature of reality. They may not have had the opportunity to study philosophy, especially

33. Plesa and Petranker, "Psychedelics and Neonihilism," 5.
34. Plesa and Petranker, "Psychedelics and Neonihilism," 6.

the field called metaphysics. Even so, they hold what can be seen as metaphysical beliefs that underlie their outlook on morality, politics, and religion. Now we are learning that psychedelics can alter these metaphysical beliefs.

Part of what makes this research especially intriguing and controversial is the fact that psychedelics change metaphysical beliefs, not just randomly or equally in all directions, but away from physicalist views and toward dualism or panpsychism. One study, which involves a single use of psychedelics, reaches this conclusion: "A single psychedelic experience increased a range of non-physicalist beliefs as well as beliefs about consciousness, meaning, and purpose."[35] Elsewhere we learn that "the great majority of participants (87%) reported that the experience changed their fundamental conception of reality. Furthermore, the percentage of participants who identified as a 'Believer (e.g., in Ultimate Reality, Higher Power, and/or God, etc.)' increased (from 29% Before to 59% After)."[36] In yet another report, we read that the "results revealed significant shifts away from 'physicalist' or 'materialist' views, and towards panpsychism and fatalism, post use."[37]

Broadly speaking, this evidence seems to support the idea that people move from naturalistic materialism to some form of idealism, dualism, or panpsychism. Most of us, however, have trouble understanding how psychedelics could possibly alter basic beliefs about metaphysics or religion. "How could a chemically induced altered state of consciousness possibly reveal metaphysical truths?"[38] What theory of drug action can explain this belief-altering effect? One explanation is based on how a psychedelic drug session can loosen our prior beliefs or ideas. We explored this briefly in chapter 3 when we looked at the REBUS model of psychedelic action. Some suggest that when psychedelics upset the grip of prior ideas and shake the mind free during a psychedelic

35. Nayak et al., "Belief Changes," 1.
36. Nayak et al., "Belief Changes," 9.
37. Timmermann et al., "Psychedelics Alter," 1.
38. Gładziejewski, "From Altered States," 3.

session, the mind is suddenly freed to consider and possibly adopt other beliefs.

The problem, however, is that the alteration of metaphysical beliefs is directional. According to the research, metaphysical beliefs are not altered randomly or evenly in every direction at once. The alterations tend to move from materialism to some form of idealism or panpsychism. By itself, REBUS can explain alteration but not directionality. "Thus, the REBUS model alone cannot explain the directional change."[39]

Another explanation is rooted in the idea that subjective experiences associated with psychedelics are felt to be meaningful, "mystical," or spiritual in their significance. Coming out of such an experience, especially in view of the "noetic" quality so often associated with the experience, people might find themselves not just loosened from prior beliefs but nudged directionally away from materialism and toward some version or other of dualism or idealism. According to one team of researchers, it is possible that "psychedelics change beliefs by producing unusually compelling experiences." If psychedelic experiences tend to be spiritual and meaningful, then it might make sense to think that they have the power to turn the direction of metaphysical ideas from materialism. If so, then it seems fair to expect that psychedelic experiences "may result in fundamental changes in the conception of reality and enduring increases in beliefs toward Dualism, spirituality, and Paranormal phenomena."[40]

Not only is there directionality in the alteration of metaphysical beliefs, but the direction of the change correlates with the mental health benefit. The more one is changed in the direction of dualism or idealism, the more one is helped in terms of mental health treatment. According to one recent study, "the belief-shifts were correlated with positive mental health changes; namely, improvements in well-being in the observational data and depression scores in the controlled research data."[41]

39. Nayak et al., "Belief Changes," 9.
40. Nayak et al., "Belief Changes," 10.
41. Timmermann et al., "Psychedelics Alter," 6.

Just because a belief is beneficial does not make it true. Perhaps psychedelics create delusions that may be good for our mental health at the expense of our intellectual integrity. Some might be willing to pay the intellectual cost of mental health, but that is not an acceptable strategy for philosophers, theologians, or anyone who is searching for the truth about how these things work. No matter how useful or comforting, and regardless of whether they come for psychedelic experiences or from the culture around us, delusions are not going to help us.

When it comes to metaphysical or religious ideas, however, who is in a position to distinguish truth from error or sound thinking from delusions? Metaphysical beliefs and religious doctrines have been debated for millennia, and good reasons can be given for and against every one of them. Of course, one can adopt a pragmatic approach developed by William James and advocated by some today. According to Jussi Jylkkä and his colleagues, we do not know whether metaphysical viewpoints such as panpsychism are delusional. We do know they can be therapeutic. "Rather than considering spiritual-type metaphysical beliefs as delusional and something to be avoided, they can be considered as part of the transformative process facilitated by psychedelic experiences."[42]

A pragmatic view would lead us to try to make the most therapeutically of whatever may be going on metaphysically. If it is true that a change in metaphysical beliefs can enhance the therapeutic effect, then supporting the therapy means supporting the alteration in metaphysical beliefs. Pointing this out, Peter Sjöstedt-Hughes suggests that some sort of metaphysics counselling might help at least some psychedelic-assisted therapy patients. He proposes that future psychedelic-assisted therapy protocols "include as an optional and additional element an intelligible metaphysical discourse" counselling opportunity.[43] Whether psychedelic-assisted therapy patients would be interested in philosophical counselling about changes in their metaphysical beliefs

---

42. Jylkkä et al., "Endorsement of Metaphysical," 17.
43. Sjöstedt-Hughes, "On the Need," 2.

is hard to predict. What might happen, however, if we substitute spiritual or religious beliefs for metaphysical?

A pragmatic argument is also advanced by a team of chaplains, who warn that leaving out the spiritual dimension may "potentially undermine treatment success." Because spirituality plays a role in the healing process, perhaps involving the alteration of metaphysical beliefs, the healing process will be strengthened for some patients when they are given spiritual and theological support. These dynamics "should be integrated" into the delivery of psychedelic-assisted therapy.[44]

Doing so may be a step too far for most providers of psychedelic-assisted therapy in the future. It is doubtful that metaphysics or spirituality will be given the consideration some claim they need, or that anyone will require or offer to pay for such support. If the need is real, as it surely will be in at least some cases, it will be met in other ways if it is met at all. Pastors, of course, are not expected to be trained in the intricacies of psychedelic-assisted therapy, and they should never pretend otherwise. Even so, perhaps by listening and offering support, local church leaders can extend the invitation of religious communities to accompany those who are wondering what just happened to them spiritually and theologically.

PSYCHEDELICS AS ENTHEOGENS

In chapter 1, we noted that some people refer to psychedelics as entheogens. The label makes sense when people use psychedelics primarily for spiritual purposes. Their spiritual intention means that they regard these drugs as sacraments or holy gifts. Research is suggesting that there are many people today who are turning to entheogens as "a form of spiritual seeking, which involves the pursuit of direct, spiritual experiences and self-realization."[45]

---

44. Palitsky et al., "Importance of Integrating," 743, 745.
45. Arnaud and Sharpe, "Entheogens and Spiritual Seeking," 76.

In the modern West, the use of psychedelics as entheogens began in the fifties. For millennia, however, the ancestors of today's indigenous communities around the world knew about the spiritual or religious value of these drugs and the experiences they bring. Despite efforts by colonial powers and church authorities to suppress the use of these drugs, traditional wisdom passed from generation to generation safeguarded the knowledge of the source of the medicines and the best ways to use them.

Throughout the world, sometimes in continuity with indigenous communities, new communities are being formed and individuals are gathering to seek psychedelic experiences that are mainly spiritual in intention. "Spiritual seekers create their own beliefs by incorporating ideas from various religious and philosophical traditions, engage in spiritual practices (e.g., meditation), place emphasis on the importance of spirituality in life, are highly open to experience, and espouse a spiritual but not religious orientation."[46]

Given the eclectic mix of traditions and styles, any effort to describe today's entheogenic scene runs into obvious challenges. The underground nature of many of these entheogenic communities compounds the problem. Broad definitions of spirituality are needed if we are to understand "how entheogenic experience relates to the religious or spiritual backgrounds of the users, as well as to their present religious or spiritual affiliations. One could study the relationship between entheogenic practices and other forms of spiritual practice such as meditation or prayer, and inquire into what forms of ritual may surround the consumption of these drugs."[47]

An example of a newly established entheogenic community is the Sacred Garden Church, based in Oakland, California. Don Lattin, a journalist who actively participated in the community, describes it as "a strange, psychedelic brew of legalization advocates, underground therapists and sincere spiritual seekers." He notes that the community calls itself "a multi-sacrament church."

46. Arnaud and Sharpe, "Entheogens and Spiritual Seeking," 70.

47. Johnstad, "Entheogenic Spirituality," 391.

In practice this means that their ceremonies use psilocybin "mushrooms, plants containing such psychedelic compounds as mescaline and DMT, and also psychoactive chemicals like MDMA and LSD."[48]

Because it is organized as a church, Sacred Garden members can claim legal protection under the First Amendment and the Religious Freedom Restoration Act. Because it is in Oakland where psychedelics are effectively decriminalized, members have few concerns about legal challenges. The community endorses the idea of "least dogma," meaning that members can adhere to the beliefs that fit their spiritual lives. In their only creedal statement, their entheogenic intent is the central component: "We are open to the possibility that, engaged through careful and respectful practice, entheogens can connect us to direct experience of the divine, within this lifetime."[49]

Individual or communal, entheogenic use is widespread around the world, according to the latest research. Among entheogenic users, drug use is infrequent, roughly three or four times a year. Various forms of use include "in group or solitary contexts, using moderate to large doses, and always reflecting upon and integrating their drug experiences into daily life."[50] When they identify spiritual experience as their intention for their psychedelic experience, users take an important first step toward spiritual transformation, Petter Johnstad suggests. He expands on this by claiming that "having a spiritual motivation for entheogen use had a powerful impact on the resulting experience, and especially so for mystical-type characteristics. Spiritually motivated entheogen users endorsed these experiential characteristics to a significantly higher extent than users without such motivation."[51]

This suggests that a clear and strong entheogenic intention is the most likely path to a profoundly meaningful spiritual experience. More than that, however, the strength and clarity of the user's

48. Lattin, *God on Psychedelics*, 121.

49. Lattin, *God on Psychedelics*, 127.

50. Arnaud and Sharpe, "Entheogens and Spiritual Seeking," 75.

51. Johnstad, "Entheogenic Spirituality," 391.

intention is key to addressing a question raised half a century ago by Huston Smith. One research team quotes Smith's challenge, written in 1964, when he said that "drugs appear able to induce religious experiences; it is less evident that they can produce religious lives."[52] Responding to Smith's challenge, the report comments by saying that "while psychedelics may evoke powerful changes in consciousness, and may promote greater openness to experience, without a clear growth or spiritually oriented motivation for use, such changes in and of themselves are unlikely to foster psychological or spiritual development."[53]

Perhaps the best reason for an entheogenic intention is provided by Johnstad: "For spiritually motivated respondents, entheogenic experiences were most commonly characterized by feelings of joy, peace, and love, by insight into oneself and one's relations, and by improved connections with nature and with other people."[54]

52. Smith, "Do Drugs Have Religious Import?" 528–29.

53. Arnaud and Sharpe, "Entheogens and Spiritual Seeking," 76–77.

54. Johnstad, "Entheogenic Spirituality," 380.

5

Mysticism and Spiritual Experience in Christianity

IN THIS CHAPTER WE turn our attention from questions about the science of psychedelics to focus on some of the most important features of mystical experience and mysticism in Christianity. What role does experience play in Christianity? In order to ask how we might think about psychedelic spirituality and its relationship to the Christianity of the future, we need first to look back at the story of spiritual experience in various strands of Christianity in the past.

The idea of spiritual and mystical experience is bigger than Christianity, and it predates the emergence of the first Christian communities. Early Christian writers picked up the word from other sources, redefining it as they began to use it to describe certain aspects of their faith, such as what happens to believers after they die or how to think about what the church came to call the sacraments. Christian mystical theology came later, and only in recent centuries have we used the words "mysticism" or "mystic" to speak of those who seem to have entered into a deeper relationship with God.

Mystical experience has been around longer than we know, but the concept of mystical experience has taken on new meanings over time, especially in the past hundred years or so. Until confusion arises, shifts in terminology can happen without anyone noticing. Christian versions of mysticism bear some resemblance to the concept of mystical experience as it is used in today's psychedelic spiritual experience research, but profound differences also exist. Matters are complicated even more by the fact that the idea of the spiritual seems more palatable to many today than the mystical. We prefer the word "spiritual" rather than "mystical," but the two terms are used here interchangeably and no significant distinction between them is made.

DEFINING MYSTICISM IN CHRISTIANITY

As valuable as it would be to have a clear definition of "Christian mysticism," nothing of the sort is available. One reason is that the idea of being a mystic is relatively new. "No mystics (at least before the present century) believed in or practiced 'mysticism.'" So writes Bernard McGinn, widely regarded as the world's leading authority on mysticism in Christianity. "The people we call mystics would have called themselves Christians," or they would have been followers of other traditions "that contained mystical elements as parts of a wider historical whole."[1]

Almost from the start, however, the Christian tradition has been home to a rich and diverse set of "spiritual practices" that are meant to prepare believers "for a deeper sense of God's presence, variously conceived of as seeing God, uniting with God, radical obedience to God, and even being annihilated in God." These practices "became integral to Christian spirituality, both in the East and the West, between 500 and 1500. This is the realm that we today call 'mysticism.'"[2]

Karl Rahner (1904–84), a foremost Catholic theologian and an acclaimed contributor to mystical theology, is also cautious about any definition that claims to be precise. He writes: "We do after all possess a vague empirical concept of Christian mysticism:

1. McGinn, *Foundations of Mysticism*, xvi.
2. McGinn, "Mysticism and the Reformation," 52.

the religious experiences of the Saints, all that they experienced of closeness to God, of higher impulses, of visions, inspirations, of the consciousness of being under the special and personal guidance of the Holy Spirit, of ecstasies," deliberately pointing to the diverse range of experiences under consideration. "All this," he says, "is comprised in our understanding of the word mysticism."[3]

Sometimes it is suggested that the essence of Christian mysticism is a search for union with God. McGinn rejects this idea, insisting that "union with God is not the most central category for understanding mysticism."[4] If not union with God, is there a better way to describe the core of Christian mysticism? McGinn prefers the word "presence." He writes: "I have come to find the term 'presence' a more central and a more useful category for grasping the unifying note in the varieties of Christian mysticism." This leads McGinn to offer a useful definition of the mystical element in Christianity. He calls it "that part of its belief and practices that concerns the preparation for, the consciousness of, and the reaction to what can be described as the immediate or direct presence of God."[5]

Outside Christianity, other mystical traditions may endorse the idea of mystical union. Christian mystics are constrained, however, by the basic theistic framework that undergirds the Christian vision. Unlike monistic traditions, Christian theism recognizes a basic and enduring ontological distinction between Creator and creatures. We human beings are creatures who are distinct from God. We are not emanations that overflow from a single source and whose destiny is to return to an original singularity. As distinct creatures, we are made to live in a loving relationship with the Creator. Our goal is not to be reabsorbed or fused with the divine. It is to enter and grow into an ever more conscious and joyous relationship with a divine reality that so often remains hidden even when its presence is felt. According to McGinn, mysticism is a "response to the presence of God, a

3. Rahner, "Ignatian Mysticism," 279–80.

4. McGinn, *Foundations of Mysticism*, xvii.

5. McGinn, *Foundations of Mysticism*, xvii.

presence that is not open, evident, or easily accessible, but that is always in some way mysterious or hidden. When that hidden presence becomes the subject of some form of immediate experience, we can perhaps begin to speak of mysticism in the proper sense of the term."[6]

In the ordinary consciousness of daily living, the presence of the divine may never be felt. But some within the Christian tradition speak or write about an "immediate consciousness of the presence of God," something that McGinn says is "a central claim that appears in almost all mystical texts."[7] In their writings, they claim that "their mode of access to God is radically different from that in ordinary consciousness, even from the awareness of God gained through the usual religious activities of prayer, sacraments, and other rituals."[8] It is not that God is unavailable to ordinary believers using ordinary means. God is present to all, "but not in any direct or immediate fashion." McGinn adds that mystical consciousness of the presence of God is different for ordinary religious consciousness because it is "both subjectively and objectively more direct, even at times as immediate."[9] McGinn elaborates on this difference: "This experience is presented as subjectively different insofar as it is affirmed as taking place on a level of the personality deeper and more fundamental than the objectifiable through the usual conscious activities of sensing, knowing, and loving."[10]

Karl Rahner, on the other hand, warns against the idea that among Christians in general there is a special class of people called mystics who have access to a deeper level of religious consciousness. Mysticism is closer to ordinary Christians than most people imagine. For Rahner, "what the mystics talk about is an experience which any Christian (and indeed any human being) can have and can seek, but which is easily overlooked or suppressed." Mysticism,

6. McGinn, "Love, Knowledge," 7

7. McGinn, *Foundations of Mysticism*, xix.

8. McGinn, *Foundations of Mysticism*, xix.

9. McGinn, *Foundations of Mysticism*, xix.

10. McGinn, *Foundations of Mysticism*, xix.

he says, "is not as remote from us as we are at first tempted to assume."[11] Notice here how Rahner claims that a mystical experience is possible not just for any Christian, but for "any human being," a claim consistent with his universalistic tendencies.

Commonplace or rare, mystical encounters in the Christian tradition are not always calm or gentle experiences. From biblical times, stories of mystical disruptions include lightning flashes, earthquakes, dark clouds, or in the case of St. Paul, getting knocked off one's horse. Mystical encounters can be costly or painful, and the reassurance of mystical consciousness might come only after all the much-loved gods of popular culture have been destroyed. When trusted gods fail, it can be the start of the mystic's path to authentic encounter. In this sense, McGinn suggests, past mystics can be today's prophets. "If the modern consciousness of God is often of an absent God (absent though not forgotten for the religious person), many mystics seem almost to have been prophets of this in their intense realization that the 'real God' becomes a possibility only when the many false gods (even the God of religion) have vanished and the frightening abyss of total nothingness is confronted."[12]

Rahner also points to the unexpected nature of the experience of grace. For him, an encounter with "God's immediate proximity" can occur "in a holy night or in blessed light, in a void silently filled by God." Those who experience grace "cannot doubt their experience of the immediate proximity of the self communicating God as effect and reality of God's sanctifying grace in the depth of their existence: in other words, as 'experience of the Holy Spirit.'"[13]

Despite the importance of the moments of subjective intensity, what defines Christian mysticism is not a special momentary experience but an entire way of life that surrounds it. McGinn writes that "it is important to remember that mysticism is always a process or way of life. Although the essential note—or better, goal—of mysticism may be conceived of as a particular kind of

11. Rahner, "Experience of the Holy Spirit," 193.

12. McGinn, *Foundations of Mysticism*, xviii.

13. Rahner "Experience of the Holy Spirit," 192.

encounter between God and the human, between Infinite Spirit and the finite human spirit, everything that leads up to and prepares for this encounter, as well as all that flows from or is supposed to flow from it for the life of the individual in the belief community, is also mystical, even if in a secondary sense."[14]

McGinn's claim that mysticism is "always a process or way of life" contrasts sharply with concepts of mysticism in William James or W. T. Stace, for whom mystical experience is everything. McGinn and Stace approach their subject matter differently, Stace as a philosopher and McGinn as one deeply attuned to the complexity of a vast literature with one faith tradition. Nevertheless, in the judgment of other experts in Christian mysticism, Stace's interpretation fails if it claims to be inclusive of Christianity. As William Wainwright puts it, "Stace's typology has been widely influential, [but] it oversimplifies and thereby distorts the richness of mystical experience."[15]

Grace Jantzen also points out the difference between traditional Christian mysticism and modern philosophical perspectives like the work of Stace. "The definition of mysticism has shifted, in modern thinking, from a patristic emphasis on the objective content of experience to the modern emphasis on the subjective psychological states or feelings of the individual."[16] She compares William James' interpretation of mysticism and religious experience with Bernard of Clairvaux and Julian of Norwich, claiming that these two "may be taken as paradigms of the Christian mystical tradition." In her view, "James' position is misguided and inadequate." The problem for us today is that it "has been of enormous influence in subsequent thinking about mysticism," affecting the work of Stace and that of psychedelic researchers trying to define and measure the link between psychedelics and mystical experience.[17]

---

14. McGinn, *Foundations of Mysticism*, xvi.

15. Wainwright, "Mysticism," 1.

16. Jantzen, "Mysticism and Experience," 295.

17. Jantzen, "Mysticism and Experience," 295.

According to Jantzen, James focused his attention on what she calls "the fringes of consciousness: psychic phenomena, hallucinations, the effects of nitrous oxide and intoxication, and intense or bizarre accounts of religious experience including trances, levitations, seizures, hallucinations, and the like."[18] She continues by pointing out that when James describes mysticism, he gives examples of "particular states of consciousness: dream-like states, trances, an experience with chloroform, flashes of exaltation, experiences of ecstatic union. These, for James, are 'mystical experiences,' and it is to experiences of these sorts that he applies his famous characteristics of ineffability, noetic quality, passivity, and transiency." These four characteristics influenced those who followed James, at least until Stace presented a longer list of qualities. Nearly everyone, however, followed the track set by James in thinking about mysticism "in terms of experiences in this narrower sense: voices, visions, ecstasies, and the like."[19]

More than James, however, it is W. T. Stace who directly influences the work of psychedelic researchers. The legacy of Stace in the MEQ is well known.[20] Whatever the strengths of Stace might be in terms of his philosophy, the adequacy of his work as an interpretation that includes Christian mysticism is widely criticized. As Wainwright puts it, "The major difficulty with an account like Stace's, however, is its failure to mention love."[21] Compare this with what McGinn has to say: "It is extremely difficult to find any Christian theology of mysticism which is not affective in the sense of giving love a crucial role in our striving toward God."[22] A contemporary of Stace, R. C. Zaehner, points to the same problem. According to Wainwright's summary of Zaehner's critique, Stace distinguishes between nature mysticism and monistic mysticism. "Nature mysticism and monistic mysticism are roughly identical with Stace's extrovertive and introvertive mysticism. Theistic

18. Jantzen, "Mysticism and Experience," 296.

19. Jantzen, "Mysticism and Experience," 302.

20. Cole-Turner, "Psychedelic Epistemology."

21. Wainwright, "Mysticism," 1.

22. McGinn, "Love, Knowledge," 12.

mysticism, on the other hand, can't be accommodated within Stace's categories." That is because "unlike monistic consciousness, theistic mystical consciousness has an object or content which is distinct from the self." The point Wainwright makes here is similar to McGinn's claim that Christian mystics seek God's presence, not union with God. According to Wainwright, "What most clearly differentiates theistic mystical consciousness from other forms of mystical experience, however, is that the nature of the relation between the mystic and the object of her experience is best indicated by the fact that she typically expresses it by employing the language of mutual love."[23]

What does this imply for research into the relationship between psychedelics and spirituality? In one sense, very little. Even if mysticism is inadequately defined in Stace, questionnaires such as the MEQ have clearly found something that people think is important, meaningful, or "spiritual." At the same time, dependence on Stace does limit the value of this research when it comes to its usefulness for Christian theology. If the definitions and measurements are not well designed in terms of the Christian mystical tradition, they can hardly be expected to measure it very well. Noting this is not meant as a complaint so much as a warning to Christians who might use this research to understand their own spirituality.

THE EXPERIENTIAL AND THE MYSTICAL IN EARLY CHRISTIANITY

"It is literally impossible to read the New Testament at any length without encountering claims that something is happening to these people, and it is happening *now*."[24] So writes Luke Timothy Johnson, a leading New Testament scholar. He continues by saying that "the New Testament writings contain an impressive amount of experiential language." Despite what seems to be so obviously

23. Wainwright, "Mysticism," 1–2.

24. Johnson, *Religious Experience*, 5; emphasis original.

true, it is also a fact that in recent centuries, Christian theologians have interpreted the Bible as if it were a collection of infallible propositional truths about God and creation. Connecting these propositions in a logical or systematic structure was the way to create doctrines. The important thing for these theologians was that the systems were logically coherent and that people believed they were the truth, not that they experienced the meaning of their truth. If it so happened that the Bible also contained experiential language, that part could be safely overlooked because it had no doctrinal significance.

Assuming that Johnson is right, how can this happen? If it is impossible to read the Bible without encountering the experiential, how is it possible to ignore it theologically while remaining Christian? It is as if a hermeneutical decision had already been made about the insignificance of experience, making it easy to ignore the theological significance of spiritual experience in the scriptures. Johnson hints at this explanation with his distinction between experiential and propositional language. "By 'experiential,' I mean language that does not serve primarily to state propositions about reality (whether with reference to God or to humans) so much as to express, refer to, and argue from human experiences. Indeed, the New Testament is remarkable among ancient religious texts for its high proportion of first-order discourse about experience."[25]

In a direct challenge to such neglect among his contemporaries, Karl Rahner packs together in a single sentence just a few texts that highlight the experiential. "Being led by the Spirit (Rom 8:14), glowing with the Spirit (Rom 12:11), being sanctified and justified in the Spirit (1 Cor 2:15; 6:11), being made to drink of the Spirit, anointed and sealed by it, creation, renewal, rebirth, strengthening, illumination (by the Spirit, Christ, grace) (Eph 3:16; Tim 1:12; 2 Tim 2:1; Eph 1:18; 5:14; Heb 6:4), etc., all these also essentially imply or embrace an inner transformation of the justified as such." Rahner follows his list with this conclusion: "The experiences expressed by these texts involve *power*."[26]

25. Johnson, *Religious Experience*, 4.
26. Rahner, "Some Implications," 320–21; emphasis original.

At the same time, we must recognize that in the Bible, experience is viewed critically. Not everything that feels like a powerful religious experience is acceptable to the community. Probably the most dramatic example of a critical stance toward the experiential is found in the oracles of the Hebrew prophets. They did more than just rail against the worship of what they called "idols." They mocked anyone who worshiped them. One famous story features the prophet, Elijah. He is outnumbered by the worshipers of Baal and Asherah, but he ridicules them publicly for their beliefs regardless of the intensity of their experience of their gods. "Elijah mocked them, saying, 'Cry aloud! Surely he is a god; either he is meditating, or he has wandered away, or he is on a journey, or perhaps he is asleep and must be awakened.'" (1 Kgs 18:27)

And who can forget the words of the prophet Amos? He warns his listeners that they had become too comfortable with their false gods and their false sense of spiritual safety. Their problem was not that they had no spiritual experiences but that their experiences were shaped by their selfish injustice. If you were to encounter the living God, he tells them, it may not go as well as you think. "Why do you want the day of the Lord? It is darkness, not light." Your gods may be happy with you, he says. But what will the true God say to you? "I hate, I despise your festivals, and I take no delight in your solemn assemblies. . . . But let justice roll down like waters, and righteousness like an ever-flowing stream" (Amos 5:20–21, 24).

The prophets are not convinced by claims just because they are based on spiritual experience. In the biblical tradition, experience may be unavoidable, but it is not infallible. By itself, experience is not enough. The obvious tension here comes from the fact that all the prophets on every side were guided by their experiences. By what standard can it be said that Elijah and Amos got it right and their opponents did not? How did they know how to distinguish what they saw as truth in their experience from the self-serving errors rooted in the experiences of others?

There is no simple answer to that question, not for us today and probably not in the time of the prophets. What this does suggest, however, is that in every time, experiences must be treated with humility and caution. Sincerity is no guarantee that our experience of God gives us true theological insight. Put another way, experience cannot serve as the criterion of its own truth. "One can hardly appeal to the Bible in support of religious experience as a criterion, given the prophetic attitude toward Israel's religious experience and Jesus' attitude toward his disciples' experience."[27] As much as experience is valued as the foundation of the life of the biblical communities, it is never taken at face value and accepted uncritically.

What, then, are the criteria by which experience is evaluated? While there is no obvious or consistent answer to that question, a process seems to be in play. Theological insight is rooted in experience, only to be reassessed over and over again by new experience, which in turn is measured against the emerging theological insights of the communities of the faithful. What is the source of this emerging insight if not the experiences of the faithful? There is an inescapable feedback loop between experience, emerging insight, critique, and more experience.

For this reason, we might wish for a place to stand outside the loop where we could have confidence in our critical principles. Is there any progress here? Is there any reason to be confident that today we are better equipped than before to test our experiences? Perhaps the best criteria for testing our spiritual experiences are the simple sayings of Amos or Micah or Jesus. Let justice roll down like waters. Do justice, love kindness, and walk humbly with your God. Love your enemies.

One can, of course, simply choose to ignore the critical insight of the community and trust entirely in the authority of one's own experience, privately interpreted. To be part of a community rooted in history, however, is to acknowledge the value of the critical insight provided by the community. To identify even broadly with the Christian community is to recognize the worth of its collective insight in guiding the interpretation of an experience with the divine. Some will fear the heavy hand of orthodoxy,

27. Thomas, "Theology and Experience," 196–97.

silencing their experiences or coercing their interpretation. They might point to the history of Christian mysticism for evidence of conflict between those who lead the church and those who are led by their experiences.

In the early church, disputes involving mysticism tended to be rare for the simple reason that the leading mystics were the leading theologians, at least through the twelfth century in the Western church. According to Bernard McGinn, "the theory of inevitable conflict between mysticism and institutional religion is challenged by the fact that so many of the key mystics in the history of Christianity have been pillars of the institution—think of Ambrose, Augustine, Gregory of Nyssa, Gregory the Great, Bernard, Bonaventure, Catherine of Siena, Gerson, Nicholas of Cusa, Ignatius of Loyola, Teresa of Avila, Thérèse of Lisieux." Instead of perpetual and "inherent opposition" between the mystics and the authorities, McGinn suggests that it is more accurate to describe the relationship as "a nuanced interaction among different elements within the framework of Catholic belief and practice."[28]

To this day, however, theories of constant conflict between mystics and clerics are commonplace in Christian circles. The theories are appealing because they reinforce a popular narrative that sees church authorities as repressive clods who are happy to marginalize the mystics rather than surrender their control. "One popular explanation is that the conflict between institutional religion and mystical piety is inevitable insofar as mysticism is based upon claims to a direct personal relation to God independent of ecclesiastical structures and mediation." McGinn mentions Don Cupitt's *Mysticism after Modernity* and its claim "that mysticism's fundamental attraction to the postmodern mentality is its subversive character—it has always been a protest against dogmatic theology and more often than not it has also served as a female critique of male-dominated religion. For Cupitt, mysticism is what saves us from religion," McGinn writes.[29]

28. McGinn, "Evil-Sounding," 200.

29. McGinn, "Evil-Sounding," 200.

Just how much truth is there to the narrative of the persecuted mystic? In Western Europe beginning in the thirteenth century, actual showdowns occurred, sometimes with tragic consequences. Wider social and institutional issues were partly to blame, as were long-standing theological debates. According to McGinn, the "conflicts between mysticism and magisterium that began around 1300 were rooted not only in the mechanisms of control evident in late medieval Christianity, but also in social aspects of the new mysticism that emerged around 1200. These new forms of mysticism were democratized, or open to all, secularized in the sense that they were realizable as much in the market place as in the cloister, and expressed for the most part in the vernacular, often by women."[30] Issues of power and social location were clearly at play, not just in conflicts involving mystics but in nearly every aspect of life in medieval Western Europe. Older church conflicts were involved as well, and some mystics were condemned as Gnostics. Some were accused of "belonging to secret groups fostering forms of knowledge in conflict with orthodoxy and not at least implicitly accessible to the wider community of faith." This was pretty much guaranteed to arouse "suspicion and often confrontation."[31]

Social forces and theological conflicts all converged in the death of Marguerite Porete (1250–1310), burned at the stake in Paris in 1310 after a trial for heresy. She was the author of *The Mirror of Simple Souls,* which in fact was anything but a simple book, although it was written in the vernacular French of her day. Porete was a member of a female lay religious order, the Beguines, which formed in northwestern Europe in the previous century. Among her teachings was the relatively new idea that the human self did not merely experience the presence of God or a state of being united with God, analogous for instance to a marriage. Nor was it that the ego is merely emptied of its self-centeredness. The new idea was that the human self must at least in some sense be destroyed or annihilated. "What was novel in the mysticism of the

30. McGinn, "Evil-Sounding," 209.
31. McGinn, "Evil-Sounding," 205.

late Middle Ages . . . was the notion of the annihilation of the self, especially of the created will."[32]

Around the same time, Meister Eckhart was tried for heresy. In the judgment of the church, he recanted his errors and lived for a few months beyond his trial. His teachings, however, were condemned for containing the idea of annihilation. Other issues were in play, but "the notion of personal annihilation took a central role."[33] The idea of mystical annihilation was upsetting to church authorities for two main reasons. First, it denied the goodness and the enduring value of the creature. Second, it seemed to suggest that the annihilated mystic, who was still very much alive, had in some sense become God. According to McGinn, "Marguerite Porete, Meister Eckhart, and later condemned mystics, like Molinos and Madame Guyon, have been accused of identifying themselves with God to the extent that they believed their actions were really God's action. The root of this mystical identity and its dangers, perceived and real, was planted in the soil of annihilation, the process of interior stripping and decreation designed to leave God alone at work, not the created person."[34]

Later mystics came close to supporting the idea of self-annihilation. Louis Dupré writes that "Saint Teresa in her description of the mystical marriage mentions an ecstasy 'so complete that it seems as though the soul no longer existed.'" A memory of the self-loss experience remains, and at least some minimal form of consciousness seems to be present before, during, and after the experience. "Hence the term 'unconscious' seems inappropriate, even though some reports refer to the unitive ecstasy as 'beyond consciousness.' Some commentators attempt to solve the problem by distinguishing consciousness from self-consciousness. Self-consciousness would be temporarily lost while consciousness remains. But how could one be at all conscious without being in some way self-conscious?"[35]

32. McGinn, "Evil-Sounding," 210.
33. McGinn, "Evil-Sounding," 207.
34. McGinn, "Evil-Sounding," 211–12.
35. Dupré, "Christian Experience," 4.

When expressed as a concept, the experience that these mystics describe as self-annihilation seems illogical and heretical. Even so, mystics such as Julian of Norwich try to describe their experiences, using the word "naughted" from the English of her time to speak of a process of becoming nothing. According to Louis Dupré, "Julian of Norwich writes: 'No soul is at rest until it has despised as nothing [naughted] all things which are created. When it by its will has become nothing [naught] for love, to have Him who is everything, then it is able to receive spiritual rest.'" Dupré points out the polarity between "naughting" and oneness with God. To become one with God is to become as nothing. "It obviously does not refer to a single act but to a slow and presumably painful process of self-emptying. Precisely at this point appears that 'dark night' which purifies the soul, beyond its own will and ability, of attachment to itself," thereby preparing one for unification.[36]

The mystic's moment of peak experience, which for some came with an intensity very much like death itself, is not well-suited for words. The experiences seem to defy expression, especially when it comes to the core question of the identity of the subject and its continuity through the experience. It is easy to see how some interpretations of experience would provoke the concerns of the guardians of orthodoxy, even if unintentionally. In the context of medieval Europe, the relationship between mystics and the church's magisterium could be complicated, sometimes being strained to the breaking point.

If there is tension between mystics and the magisterium, another kind of strain manifests itself in the relationship between mystics and the masses. From the earliest days of Christianity until today, it is not entirely clear how to connect the unusual experiences of the mystics with the less intense spiritual lives of ordinary believers. Central to the Christian message from the beginning is that all are invited to enter into a saving relationship with God through the church, especially through the sacraments or "mysteries." Everyone balked at the idea that mystics are a

36. Dupré, "Christian Experience," 6.

kind of spiritual elite, as if they alone have a premier level access to God that is not open to all. Ordinary Christian experience is fully adequate for salvation and for full participation in the life of the community. And yet the problem remains as long as intense spiritual experiences remain. The challenge is to identify "where exactly the Christian mystical experience differs from the Christian religious experience."[37]

For us today, of course, the problem takes on a new complexity. Are Christians who have spiritual experiences, especially psychedelic spiritual experiences, different from other Christians?

PROTESTANTS AND MYSTICS

Often it is said that ever since Martin Luther (1483–1546), Protestants have rejected mysticism. Experts tend to agree that Luther's own views on mysticism were complicated. It is true that he was not a mystic in anything like the usual sense. What McGinn calls "the mystical element," however, is clearly present in his thought. The reformer drew on "re-interpreted aspects of mysticism within the context of his new evangelical theology. Luther read the mystics selectively for the purpose of finding support for his own theology."[38] In fact, central to the core of Protestantism is a "stress on the need for inner experience of God as the foundation for true faith, and an emphasis on humility and passivity while waiting for God's justifying grace."[39]

Also central to the Protestant movement, however, is an insistence on the importance of the Scriptures as the only trustworthy foundation for the theology of the church. Luther himself translated the entire Bible into German, an extraordinary feat of scholarship and cultural significance. Luther's Bible was printed using the Guttenberg method by printers all over Europe, who brought the scriptures and other religious texts to people of modest

37. Sells, "From a History," 392.

38. McGinn, "Mysticism and the Reformation," 54.

39. McGinn, "Mysticism and the Reformation," 55.

means. In the earliest years of the Reformation, the interpretation of scripture or exegesis was combined with practical experience to shape the new movement. "Martin Luther developed his theology of justification by faith through a process of reciprocal interpretation between exegesis and experience, and argued that 'experience alone makes the theologian,'" according to Simeon Zahl.[40]

Early in the Reformation, Luther's openness to the importance of the spiritual experience was tested when some of his followers, such as Andreas Karlstadt (1486–1541), took things far beyond what Luther himself wanted. For Luther, any insight from experience must always be guided and constrained by the scriptures, rightly interpreted. Karlstadt, Luther came to think, had an exaggerated sense of the clarity with which he thought he heard the unmediated voice of the Holy Spirit. According to Zahl, "Luther came to believe that the theological essence of Karlstadt's position, like that of other 'enthusiasts,' is a privileging of inner experience, interpreted as experience of God's Spirit, over the external instruments of the Bible and the biblically authorized sacraments. This theology seems to have touched a deep nerve in Luther, and he accused Karlstadt and others like him of 'devouring the Holy Spirit, feathers and all.'"[41] In response to Karlstadt, Luther moved to a "new, pessimistic view on subjective experience."[42]

If Luther shifted toward greater suspicion regarding experience and mysticism, other leading reformers like John Calvin (1509–1566) were also cautious because of the doctrinal supremacy they attached to the scriptures. McGinn thinks that Calvin was more negative toward mysticism than Luther, although he left behind a mixed legacy. "The Reformers, though in different ways, sought to come to terms with the rich traditions of Christian mysticism, adopting some aspects, rejecting others, and more often effecting transformations in what they had inherited."[43] In the next century or so, as Protestant theology became more

---

40. Zahl, *Holy Spirit*, 10.

41. Zahl, *Holy Spirit*, 27.

42. Zahl, *Holy Spirit*, 21.

43. McGinn, "Mysticism and the Reformation," 56.

systematic and rationalistic, the mystical element was pushed to the edges. The official confessions of Protestant Orthodoxy tended to ignore the mystical. Nevertheless, the reformers themselves drew deeply on the ancient Christian tradition, reserving a place within Protestantism for "the spirituality and mysticism of the patristic and medieval heritage they inherited."[44]

Almost from the start, Protestants divided themselves from each other to create various branches and new movements, giving rise to what are now countless denominations and national churches. One of these early movements was known as pietism. Reacting to what they saw as doctrinal rigidity, pietist groups emerged throughout the Protestant territories of northern Europe, stressing what they claimed were the essentials of Christian living over doctrinal technicalities, thereby putting experience above intellectualism.

In terms of global impact, the most important leader in the pietist movement was John Wesley (1703–91). As a young churchman, Wesley was exposed to those who advocated "inward religion," something we would call spirituality. Inward religion "was not an unfamiliar theme to devout Christians of Wesley's age. Anglican divines, Catholic mystics, Puritans, German Pietists and English Quakers were all concerned with inward religion or experimental Christianity." Wesley's own parents were part of the movement. His mother had a profound impact on his thinking, and "his father's dying words were 'the inward witness, the inward witness.'"[45] These influences led Wesley to turn to his own experience and to develop the importance of the shared life of spiritual experience as the defining core of the Wesleyan movement, known in many places as the "Methodist" church.

Wesley was hardly alone in calling attention to the importance of spiritual experience in the Christian life. Jonathan Edwards (1703–58) emphasized some of the same themes in the North American colonial context. His intellectual achievements are highly regarded to this day, and his preaching helped to lead

44. McGinn, "Mysticism and the Reformation," 61.
45. Del Colle, "John Wesley's Doctrine," 174.

to the First Great Awakening or Evangelical Revival, a kind of mass movement of pietism among Protestants on both sides of the Atlantic. In the United States, a Second and a Third Awakening followed in the eighteenth and nineteenth centuries, permanently shaping the religious character of American Protestantism in the direction of pietism and evangelicalism.

The Evangelical Protestantism prominent in nineteenth- and twentieth-century American Christianity placed great emphasis on the importance of personal spiritual experience. To be a Christian, one must undergo a conversion experience, a conscious act of repentance or turning away from a former life in order to begin a new kind of life through a process of being "born again." Evangelical Protestants also kept alive the Reformers' view of the primacy of scripture as the most reliable source of theology, often merging it with an idea of biblical inerrancy on the one hand and the dogmas of Protestant Orthodoxy on the other. Their emphasis on the necessity of experience continued, but increasingly their idea of experience was reduced to a narrowly prescribed conversion narrative of a sinner saved by grace. Whatever truth is contained in the formula became distorted when it was pressed upon people as the only acceptable path. Even where Evangelicalism remained a rich and experientially vibrant tradition, it has fallen under the spell of American politics since the eighties. Candidates for office routinely seek the support of Evangelicals, and increasingly the movement is defined by its conservative politics and not by its championing of the experiential in theology.

Pentecostal and charismatic movements, rooted somewhat in historical Evangelical Protestantism but with a bold emphasis on the collective experience of the presence of the Holy Spirit, hold to the importance of experience as a source of theology. Although they are largely marginalized in academic theology, they have begun to develop a new theology of the presence and power of the Spirit in the church. Pentecostal churches are growing in numbers throughout the world, especially in Latin America and Africa.

REJECTING EXPERIENCE

The impact of thinkers such as Nietzsche, Feuerbach, Marx, and Freud ushered in new levels of critical awareness in the modern West. Theological appeals to experience were suddenly suspect. "An unqualified appeal to experience is thus seen as naive unless the social, psychological, and philosophical determinants of experience are exposed."[46] In that environment, Christian theologians became suspicious of their own theological achievements and those of the past. They recognized that Christian theology over the ages was entangled with violence and injustice. When Christians accommodate evil and use their theology to justify it, can any part of their theology be trusted? When they support their beliefs by their experiences, can religious experience ever be trusted as self-validating? The conclusion seemed unavoidable. "The great variety and instability of Christian experience, including its fascist, racist, sexist, and classist forms, hardly qualifies it to function as a theological criterion."[47]

It was fascism of the thirties, following so quickly on the heels of the support voiced by leaders in the German churches for World War I, that prompted Karl Barth's attack on theology based on human experience. Barth was hardly the first modern Protestant to reject mysticism. His teachers, whom he criticized for supporting World War I, were themselves critical of mysticism. According to McGinn, "Von Harnack's opposition between Protestantism and mysticism was rooted in the theological tradition of Albrecht Ritschl (1822–89) and his followers, and also found expression in the dialectical theology of Karl Barth (1886–1968) and Emil Brunner (1889–1966). It is still strong in some Protestant circles today."[48] As McGinn points out, the nineteenth century Protestant historians held "a flawed monolithic view of mysticism." They tended to see it as a Greek philosophical intrusion into Christianity. Its goal was a kind of union with God that bordered on the idea

46. Schner, "Appeal to Experience," 42.
47. Thomas, "Theology and Experience," 196–97.
48. McGinn, "Mysticism and the Reformation," 50–51.

of a "'mingling' of the divine and the human."[49] Here again, we see McGinn pointing to the contrast that he draws between union with God and the more distinctively Christian mystical view of the felt presence of God. The problem is not that Ritschl and Harnack rejected mystical union but that they misinterpreted it as Christian mysticism.

Barth went further than his predecessors in his rejection of the role of subjective experience in theology, and his influence has had lasting consequences for Protestant theology. According to Zahl, "Barth has done more to problematize the category of 'experience' for later theology than any figure since Luther."[50] In Protestant academic circles, the theological critique of experience has dominated intellectual trends for decades.

Outside Protestant academic circles, there has always been a reaction to the rejection of the importance of experience for everyday Christianity. Some Protestants found a spiritual home for themselves in Evangelical or Pentecostal churches. Others took it for granted that their own tradition had done such a complete job of rejecting mystical and spiritual experience that anyone looking for it today must look outside the ordinary Protestant denominations. Some turned to Catholics for help, not to convert to Catholicism but to tap into a tradition that seemed to welcome spiritual experience. Others turned to Celtic Christianity, with its embrace of the daily rhythms of the natural world as points of contact, so-called "thin places" where the divine is close and God's presence can be felt. Others, of course, left the church altogether or turned to sources outside Christianity.

Among academic theologians, the critique offered by Barth has been largely persuasive. Human experience cannot be allowed to contribute as a source to our theological perspective. According to Zahl, Barth and others insisted that we must draw "our theology from external sources like the Bible or church tradition rather than from experience or self-reflection."[51] Only then will we have

49. McGinn, "Mysticism and the Reformation," 51.

50. Zahl, *Holy Spirit*, 31.

51. Zahl, "Anglican Theology," 442.

a sure foundation, intellectually speaking. But is it possible to have a theology that is truly independent of the lived experience of the theologian? Of course not, Zahl argues. No matter how much theologians want to believe that their perspective is free of the taint of their own subjective experience, they are deluding themselves if they think that "their theology is not implicitly shaped, constantly and profoundly, by their personal histories, their feelings, the social contexts, and so on."[52]

Not only does experience shape the ideas put forward by theological scholars; it also should inform the meaning of the Christian faith for academic theologians and ordinary believers alike. With that conviction in mind, Zahl offers an incisive critique of the theology of T. F. Torrance and Kathryn Tanner. According to Zahl, these two theologians rightly emphasize the idea that the meaning of human salvation is found in our participation in Christ. Both, however, make what Zahl calls "a swerve away from experience in favor of ontological categories."[53] Zahl is not rejecting the notion of an ontological dimension of the meaning of salvation. He agrees with Torrance and Tanner about the objective truth of a real relationship between the human and the divine secured by our participation by grace in Christ.

Where they fail, he believes, is in their denial of the experiential. They think the work of salvation "can be described reliably only through ontological rather than experiential categories." The Holy Spirit can be at work in you "without [your] experiencing anything that is practically recognizable to others or indeed to yourself, beyond the sheer, bald fact of baptism."[54] They may be formally correct when they say that the Spirit makes salvation real to us. But in what ways does the transformative encounter register at all in conscious awareness? "Does it manifest primarily affectively, in our feelings, or cognitively, in the way we think, or noetically, in what and how we know, or relationally, in the character and quality of our relationships to others, or what? How does

52. Zahl, "Anglican Theology," 442.

53. Zahl, *Holy Spirit*, 71.

54. Zahl, *Holy Spirit*, 107.

participating in the eucharist actually change us in ways that might be observable in the world over time?"[55]

The attempted rejection of experience in the theologies of Torrance and Tanner leads Zahl to make a stinging criticism: "Torrance's soteriology ends up operating, in practice, at the level of pure conceptuality. It functions as a kind of pneumatological Docetism," alluding to an early Christian heresy that denied the reality of the incarnation in human flesh.[56] Without a doubt, Torrance would have been horrified at the thought that his theology was in any way docetic.

Whether Zahl's criticisms will stand the test of time remains to be seen. Some will agree with Scott MacDougall: "There is no question in my mind that the dynamic Zahl has identified is one that plagues academic theology. For the reasons Zahl names, plus more besides, theologians often decline to take experience and affect as seriously as we ought, though that is changing, as Zahl himself points out. This is a salutary thing, indeed."[57]

Others may be more cautious. There seems to be no question in anyone's mind, however, that Christianity is in decline in the modern West. Could its decline be connected to its rejection of the importance of spiritual experience, especially in today's culture where people seem to value the spiritual over the religious? Churches today might score high marks for their social activism and their community engagement. What would it be like, however, for churches to provide opportunities for spiritual growth, actively nurturing spiritual experiences however they may happen?

RETURNING TO EXPERIENCE

Around the time of Vatican II (1962–65), theological observers started to call attention to a return to experience as a source of inspiration and understanding. In 1973, Anne Carr wrote that

---

55. Zahl, *Holy Spirit*, 73.

56. Zahl, *Holy Spirit*, 99.

57. MacDougall, "On the Theological Status," 433.

"human experience itself has become an explicit source in Catholic theology."[58] Pointing to the same trend, Owen Thomas tied it to broader cultural movements and expresses concern about where it is headed. According to Thomas, "contemporary theologians are talking a great deal about experience . . . without much clarity or precision. This is probably the result of the swing of the theological pendulum to the left in the latter half of this century. It is also probably determined by the 'hunger for experience' (Gadamer, Biersdorf) which has emerged in Western culture since the sixties. This in turn I take to be an aspect of a contemporary romantic movement."[59]

More recently, MacDougall writes about the students he is seeing in his seminary classroom. In response to Zahl, MacDougall claims that students walk in already believing that experience is important to Christian life and thought. In fact, they "find it very difficult to perceive the thrust of Barth's worries, which is perplexing, given the extent to which so much Christianity in the United States exemplifies his concerns." They are not afraid to use experience as a source for their theological convictions. Their problem, he says, is that "they are often quite happy to consider experience to be a source, sometimes even a primary source, and in very rare instances, even the only source for Christian theological reasoning."[60] Formed as they are by today's culture, seminary students according to MacDougall are "almost pre-programmed to elevate it [experience] to authoritative status by the time they come to study theology in a disciplinary sense." Far from marginalizing experience, these students seem eager to grant it the role of "the outsized theological authority."[61] Whether or not MacDougall is entirely fair to his students, his warning is a useful reminder that in the Christian tradition, experience is never granted uncritical acceptance as a theological authority.

58. Carr, "Theology and Experience," 359.

59. Thomas, "Theology and Experience," 179.

60. MacDougall, "On the Theological Status," 433.

61. MacDougall, "On the Theological Status," 433.

Experience informs theology, but experience is shaped and informed by culture. MacDougall is right that experience is prized in our culture. It is not just valued as a source of wisdom but claimed as a base for personal authority. Cameras are everywhere, not so much to take pictures of the scenery or the people in front of us but to take "selfies" that memorialize the moment of personal experience. The photographer's face in the foreground is more significant than the scene in the background. Being there is more important than what is out there. The scene is only worth recording because the face makes the meaning.

If we want to draw upon experience as a source of theological understanding, how do we understand experience? How do we avoid the equivalent of theological selfies? How do we keep our experience of the presence of God from defining the meaning of God? Part of the answer lies in a willingness to understand and interpret the meaning of our experiences in the light of the best guidance we can find. For someone who identifies with Christianity, this means entering into the mutually critical feedback loop between experience, emerging insight, critique, and more experience that defines the Christian community at its best. It is to embrace the best criteria of our tradition, simple as they may be. Doing so is part of experience itself, understood not as a flash of intense encounter but as the flow of events before, during, and after what the peak of intensity may have been. As Bernard McGinn noted, mysticism is "always a process or way of life."

The idea of experience as a process is developed in the writings of David Lamberth. He suggests that it is helpful to distinguish between three views of religious experience. The first, often attributed to James, is called the "evidential" use. According to Lamberth, some scholars have tried to show "how particular religious experiences, taken analogously to moments of sense perception, can be understood to found, ground, justify, or otherwise produce veridical knowledge claims about the divine."[62] Even though the evidential use is inspired by James and his views of the noetic quality of mystical experiences, it overlooks what James

62. Lamberth, "Putting 'Experience' to the Test," 68–69.

actually says about the lack of any public value to the truth-claims that might follow from a mystical experience. The experience can seem more real than ordinary reality, and its insights more profound and true, but no claim of publicly authoritative truth can be made.

Lamberth contrasts the evidential use of experience with a view that is often called "contextualist." This view derives from criticisms made by Steven Katz and others of James and Stace, especially their perennialism. Contextualists argue that there are no unmediated experiences. Religious experiences are always structured by the experiencer's context. Any religious experience is entirely or "objectively over-determined by the contexts and practices linguistic—and otherwise—that precede and provide the setting for it." Religious experience is not an unmediated encounter with the holy. It always follows "from pre-existing religious claims and contexts."[63]

Drawing on while also rejecting the first two views, Lamberth suggests that there is a third way to think about experience. It is indebted to the work of the American philosopher Charles Sanders Peirce and to the essays of Ralph Waldo Emerson. The defining feature of the third view is how it understands the nature of experience itself, not as a momentary flash of perception or sensation, but as a lived process. In Lamberth's interpretation, "Experience is not the same as perception, which is, among other things, singular in time. Experience . . . is an event, one accessible only mediately, or upon reflection, rather than directly through perception or sensation. Further, for Peirce experience is complex and inferential by nature, involving intellectual composition, discriminatory association, and conceptual and contextual construction."[64]

As an event or process, experience has a flow to it from its beginning to middle to end. It includes perception or sensation, but it is not sensation by itself, much less a kind of raw or unmediated sensation. As a process, "Experience is by its nature

63. Lamberth, "Putting 'Experience' to the Test," 69.
64. Lamberth, "Putting 'Experience' to the Test," 70.

interpretive."[65] While the constructivist view may downplay the significance of the role of sensation or perception, it is correct in arguing that experience is not naked perception. Lamberth endorses "the constitutive interweaving of the perceptual with the rational or inferential, and thus the constructed character of all experience, whether conforming to sensation or not. This sort of constructivist insight, it seems to me, itself undergirds the recognitions of many in and out of the study of religion concerning the impossibility of sufficiently founding particular religious claims via discrete religious experience."[66] At the same time, Lamberth steers clear of what he sees as constructivist reductionism, the view that religious experience is nothing more than the context of the experiencer. He holds open the more traditional, commonsense idea that experiences can be "communicative" with "distinctive aspects of reality."[67]

Central to Lamberth's view is that our lives are experiential, not in the sense that we have moments of experience that happen to us, but that we are always in the flow of experiencing. He draws on Emerson to redefine the meaning of experience and the experiential:

> Life is not so much made up of experiences as life is experiential. That is, experience is not something we have now and again, but rather something constitutively environmental, something we stand, think, and move both in and with. From this it follows that particular experiences as we speak of them do not directly give rise to singular expressions, or particular knowledge. Rather, experience flows and interfuses, always changing, making difficult our quests for vision and insight, groggy as we are due to our heavy droughts of lethe, the effects of which never ebb, even in the noonday sun. Experience is, for Emerson, the substance of our lives, but it is never radiant. We see through a glass darkly.[68]

65. Lamberth, "Putting 'Experience' to the Test," 70.
66. Lamberth, "Putting 'Experience' to the Test," 70.
67. Lamberth, "Putting 'Experience' to the Test," 71.
68. Lamberth, "Putting 'Experience' to the Test," 73.

Our idea of the experiential, Lamberth suggests, draws on the etymology of the word "experience." In Latin, the verb *experiri* means "to try or to test" in the sense of the "trials and tests of faith recounted from earliest biblical times."[69] So often in popular Christianity, people speak or sometimes sing of being "tested and tried," as if to say that the complexities of their spiritual experiences are not easily understood. Spiritual experiences are tests and trials for the faithful, and the faithful test their experiences by the shared wisdom of the community. Nothing about it is straightforward or easy.

Circling back once more to James, Lamberth speaks of experience "as a tumbling of ocean waves or a succession of waves of experience." It is not "an orderly or controlled process of knowing, whether religious or scientific. Instead, it calls affectively to mind the fact that our conscious and interpretive lives are but partial, subject to powers and structures that limit and affect us, but also constitute our lives as what they are."[70]

Perhaps the best description, however, comes from Lamberth's recounting of Emerson's view. "Experience is not simply a warrant for faith, or a warrant for particular claims or explanations; rather experience is faith's context and substance, its inescapable collaborator, its inquisitor, and also its gentle guide, offering disclosure, however unclear, of the wonder within which we find our lives."[71]

69. Lamberth, "Putting 'Experience' to the Test," 74.
70. Lamberth, "Putting 'Experience' to the Test," 77.
71. Lamberth, "Putting 'Experience' to the Test," 75.

6

Psychedelics and a Theology of Spiritual Experience

A RECENT POLL BY the Pew Research Center looked at the those who identify as "nones," defined as people who say they are "religiously unaffiliated, describing themselves as atheists, agnostics or 'nothing in particular' when asked about their religion."[1] As a group, the "nones" account for 28 percent of the adult population in the United States. Half of them say they are spiritual, but they avoid religious affiliation. When asked why, their top reason is that they "dislike religious organizations." The second most common reason was given by 30 percent of the respondents, who said that "bad experiences they've had with religious people help explain why they are nonreligious."[2]

What this suggests is that as much as church-going Christians might distrust the spirituality of people who use psychedelics, those who use psychedelics or find other pathways to spirituality may have even stronger reasons to stay away from traditional Christians. In a climate of mutual suspicions, what can possibly be gained by offering a Christian interpretation of psychedelic

1. Pew Research Center, "Religious 'Nones' in America," 6.
2. Pew Research Center, "Religious 'Nones' in America," 9.

spiritual experiences? Some will see the task as a failure from the start because nobody wants it.

It would be helpful if we had data on the question of whether psychedelic experiences tend to awaken an interest in Christianity. Based on anecdotal information, it seems safe to believe that at least a few people say that their drug experience did more than kindle a generic spirituality. It got them thinking specifically about whether Christianity might have something to offer. Perhaps they grew up with a connection with a Christian church. Scandals or bad experiences or just plain boredom made them want to leave, as many millions have done in recent decades. Then, perhaps because of a psychedelic experience, they began a new search for spiritual connections. As they integrated the meaning of the intense moment of their drug experience with the broader meaning of their lives, new questions began to arise. Was their experience anything more than just a weird or puzzling moment? Did the sense of a transcendent presence point to anything that might be real?

Pew also found that 38 percent of the "nones" say that at least once in their lives, they "experienced a 'sudden or unexpected feeling of connection with something from beyond this world,' while 25% say they feel the presence of something beyond this world at least several times a year."[3] The survey also found that "49% of 'nones' say they think of themselves as spiritual or that spirituality is very important in their lives."[4] Pew did not ask about psychedelics, so we do not know how often drugs play a role in the spiritual experiences of the "nones," but it seems likely that some of them were using psychedelics when their experiences occurred.

When it comes to the question of whether psychedelic spiritual experiences can be interpreted as part of a Christian life, churches and their leaders are likely to respond in various ways. Brian Macallan suggests four possibilities. "The first response is that which sees these experiences as illusions." Some, he suggests, will interpret spiritual experiences that occur outside the church

3. Pew Research Center, "Religious 'Nones' in America," 66.

4. Pew Research Center, "Religious 'Nones' in America," 61.

"as inherently evil." Others might offer a completely different interpretation, claiming that any spiritual experience involving psychedelic-assisted therapy, whether the patient wants it or not, is an "encounter [with] the Christian God." Macallan's fourth option is to recognize that spiritual experiences are "not exclusive to the Christian tradition." He says that anyone who has a psychedelic spiritual experience, "if they wish, can interpret their experiences as consistent with their Christian belief."[5]

How do we interpret psychedelic spiritual experiences as consistent with Christian belief? Who does the interpreting? The person with the experience, or the wider Christian community? Macallan seems to imply that it is the person with the experience who is in the position to interpret the experience as consistent with Christianity. While that is true, the wider community is also called on to offer its perspective, not to presume to offer instruction or to answer for others, but to explore possibilities for interpretation that draw on the resources of Christianity over the ages, offering them as suggestions for consideration. It is up to those with psychedelic spiritual experiences to draw on what the community has to offer, both in terms of its ideas and its offer of support. As much as it is up to the individual to interpret a personal psychedelic spiritual experience as consistent with Christian belief, it is clearly the task of the wider Christian community to integrate some of the common or shared features of psychedelic spiritual experiences with Christian perspectives.

What steps are involved here? First, we review the key features of spiritual experiences, including psychedelic spiritual experiences, done in a way that connects each point with theological insights from the Christian tradition. While using their own words, people who claim to have psychedelic spiritual experiences use terms that can be clustered together by researchers who are looking for similarities and patterns. What we learn from this process is that spiritual experiences are varied and embodied. They can be disruptive moments and transformative processes. They are

5. Macallan, "Christian Responses," 5–6.

numinous and meaningful, so much so that they tend to change the fundamental views of reality for those who have them.

Each of these terms has deep theological resonance within Christianity. In the end, what this suggests for Christian theology is that spiritual experiences, including those that occur when psychedelic drugs are involved, can be interpreted not just as minimally compatible with Christian beliefs, but as an enriching contribution, at least for some. They can be seen as accessible entrance points and pathways to authentic spiritual growth.

VARIED AND EMBODIED

Spiritual experiences are varied. William James claimed as much in the very title of his book, *The Varieties of Religious Experience*, a point repeated by Yaden and Newberg. Variability in spiritual experiences is a claim for which there is theological support. Rahner argues that "the New Testament is aware also of sublime experiences of the Spirit in the most varied forms, which can be summed up under the heading of 'mysticism.'"[6] It is as if the variation in spiritual experience that originates from human diversity is matched and multiplied by the diversifying work of the Holy Spirit. Zahl argues in a similar way that in a Christian view the "experience of the Spirit is irreducibly pluriform and particular, encompassing not only the dramatic and episodic (e.g., conversion experiences), but also the Spirit's involvement in longer term affective-dispositional change . . . [and in] instances of guidance, gifting, calling, and healing."[7] In that sense, theology's notion of diversity as originating in the Spirit is broad-ranging, including not just intense experiences in all their forms but the less dramatic, more everyday encounters that sustain spirituality over time. While psychedelic spiritual experiences are often intense, one of their functions may be to awaken one to an awareness of the many

6. Rahner, "Experience of the Holy Spirit," 207–8.
7. Zahl, *Holy Spirit*, 53.

experiences of lesser intensity but no less spiritual meaning that occur every day.

Different cultures, different personalities, and different times in our lives can all contribute to the variations in spiritual experiences. Taken together, in fact, all this suggests yet another dimension of variation, which we might call the "variety of interpretations." Not only is there a variety of spiritual experiences, as Yaden and Newberg suggest, but a variety of interpretations that can be given to any single experience. One person might interpret an experience as consistent with Christian faith while another might interpret a similar experience using another philosophical or spiritual tradition altogether.

Science and theology agree that spiritual experiences are embodied events. They may be described as "mental events," but they are never merely intellectual or rational or lacking in the dynamics of the body-brain relationship. Recent theology is generally in agreement with the importance of human embodiment as basic to our view of humanity. In the past century, many theologians have turned away from a body-soul dualism. One reason is that it is generally acknowledged that the biblical texts portray the human person as a psychosomatic unity. The scriptures describe our relationship with God in terms that include every dimension of our humanity. The rejection of body-soul dualism is not a denial of the importance of human mental activity as having causal significance. While backing away from metaphysical dualism, theologians have turned to various theories from panpsychism to emergence theory as explanations for the possibility of mental action without dualism.

What we are learning about psychedelic spiritual experiences can be seen as reinforcing the trend in theology away from dualism. The scientific study of the embodied nature of spiritual experiences connects us theologically with the belief that human beings are psychosomatic unities. It is as if the science of spiritual experiences is suggesting two things at once for consideration in Christian theology. The first is that we should stop ignoring spiritual experiences. The second is that we should stop ignoring the body and its essential place in the multilevel complexity of the human person.

DISRUPTIVE MOMENTS AND TRANSFORMATIVE PROCESSES

Thinking of experiences as processes rather than as discrete moments is especially helpful when we try to make sense of psychedelic experience. In chapter 3, we noticed how psychedelic experiences can be fast acting and long lasting. They involve a peak period that is normally a few hours long when the drug is active in the patient's brain and body. After the peak has passed, the changes caused by these drugs continue to cause secondary changes in the body and brain for weeks at least, with effects that can last a lifetime. What is this "experience" if not a process? It may include a peak moment of highest intensity that can be time-stamped on a calendar, but the experience outlasts its peak. Its full meaning can only be discovered over time, if at all.

Calling attention to the downstream consequences of these drugs should not make us lose sight of their suddenness. Psychedelics can be disruptive. They can sweep over us suddenly in a way that is unsettling and transformative. In chapters 3 and 4, we saw some of the ways in which psychedelics act on our bodies and brains, relaxing our beliefs. The REBUS theory is now expanded with the proposal that something like entropy happens in the heart when its rhythms become less organized. REBUS and the "entropic heart" have been suggested as ways to understand the intense, whole-body disruption of the psychedelic experience. What stands out here is that psychedelic experiences are fast and slow, at once disruptive and transformative.

The Christian tradition recognizes that there is such a thing as sudden or disruptive spiritual change. A problem in contemporary academic theology, however, is that the most widely embraced theory of spiritual change is grounded in virtue theory and in the idea of the formation of habits and habitus. Whatever contributions this theory makes to theology, it is not very good in helping us understand rapid changes. Zahl writes that "the concept of habitus is not very useful for explaining relatively rapid changes in individuals or groups."[8] He continues by speaking of "relatively short-duration, often affective, dimensions of Christian encounter with grace" as commonplace in the biblical writers like Paul.[9] When theologians think about spiritual change, most often they think of it as a slow process. Theologies based on virtue theory may be helpful in explaining how a slow process of transformation can take shape in a believer's life by repeating the practices of the Christian community. But can they explain profound spiritual changes that occur suddenly? Theologically speaking, is sudden spiritual change even possible? And if theology cannot explain it, are Christians being encouraged to look for it or to welcome it when it happens?

Just because a spiritual experience may be sudden or disruptive does not make it any less a part of a larger process. What happens suddenly or unexpectedly may have lasting impact. An event may come on quickly and unexpectedly, but its effects may linger for a lifetime. The transformation can be so profound that the person feels like a different person, perhaps like a new person or as the "person I was always meant to be." According to Yaden and Newberg, "it appears that the impact of some spiritual experiences is so great that the individual becomes an altogether new self—that is, some spiritual experiences can be transformative."[10] A few pages later, referring to the ideas of William James, they note that "spiritual experiences can result in persisting positive effects as well as the sense that one has become a new self, which can sometimes even last a lifetime."[11]

In traditional Evangelical Protestantism, sudden spiritual change was often held up as the paradigmatic form of change, often described as a conversion or a process of being born again. Drawing on the earlier traditions of pietism and the teachings of Wesley,

8. Zahl, "Incongruous Grace," 68.

9. Zahl, "Incongruous Grace," 70.

10. Yaden and Newberg, *Varieties*, 328.

11. Yaden and Newberg, *Varieties*, 330.

Zahl is open to the idea of sudden, intense, and transformative encounters with the Spirit as one form of transformation among others. He calls for theology to recognize "the power, legitimacy, and theological significance of dramatic and irruptive experiences of the Spirit." He points to the limits of virtue theory to account fully for disruptiveness of spiritual experiences, arguing "that one of the chief problems with habit-based accounts of sanctification is their inability to make sense of more rapid transformations wrought by the Spirit in human lives."[12]

Christian traditions vary on how they describe spiritual transformation or speak of becoming "a new self." While evangelicals use language like this, often saying that the transformation process involves being "born again," those in the older traditions within Protestantism and most Catholic Christians tend to point to instruction or catechesis as the best way to move forward through a process of spiritual reorientation. All Christian groups, however, share some anxiety about how likely the spiritual transformation of individuals is to take root and last over time.

From the context of science rather than theology, Yaden and Newberg raise some of the same questions. "There is a big question remaining when it comes to the transformations that can result from intense spiritual experiences: How do long-lasting changes occur from such a short experience?" They are not denying that sudden changes can occur. They are simply calling attention to the lack of a good theory about how this can happen, an explanatory lacuna that science seems to share with theology. "Since these experiences can occur over a time period of mere minutes, how does the brain undergo such a radical and long-lasting shift so quickly? The brain typically does not substantially alter its long-term functioning on such a short timescale." They see no easy answers, just unanswered questions that call for "additional research on how spiritual experiences sometimes make lasting transformations possible."[13]

12. Zahl, "Affective Augustinianism," 167.

13. Yaden and Newberg, *Varieties*, 341–42.

Some help in thinking about how intense moments can have lasting effects can be found in remembering that experience is a process. David Lamberth's ideas along these lines, briefly described in chapter 5, are particularly useful. It may also help us to recall the intensity of spiritual experiences themselves, especially their numinous quality, their meaningfulness, and their tendency to alter metaphysical beliefs. What do these features suggest for a Christian view of spiritual experience?

THE NUMINOUS, THE MEANINGFUL, AND THE METAPHYSICAL

In chapter 4, we saw how Yaden and Newberg refer to the numinous as the prototypical spiritual experience, saying that it is "among the most prevalent and impactful spiritual experiences."[14] People with mystical experiences tend most often to refer to them as "the feeling of being in touch with divinity." Speaking as scientists, however, they back away from making any philosophical or theological assessment of the objective validity of the feeling of the presence of God. They appeal instead to "a sense of epistemic humility regarding spiritual experiences" when it comes to the question of the actual existence of the reality whose presence is felt. "These experiences touch on life's biggest mysteries, our most heartfelt feelings, and our most profound sense of reality itself."[15]

Theology must also be humble about the question of the existence of God. Theologians cannot claim to know or prove that there is a God by appealing to philosophy or scripture. We can point to the confession of Christians over time, not to confirm that God exists but to show that people in this community have lived and died with a belief in the reality of what they experience spiritually. What theology claims is that Christianity confesses belief in a God who is available to human beings through the presence of the Holy Spirit. Christian mystical or experiential theology is rooted in the

14. Yaden and Newberg, *Varieties*, 182.
15. Yaden and Newberg, *Varieties*, 400–401.

conviction that our spiritual experiences of divine presence can correspond to the reality of the presence of God. Where Yaden and Newberg define numinous spiritual experience as "the feeling of being in touch with divinity or God," the Christian believer adds, without proof and yet with a sense of confidence that goes beyond human explanation, that the "feeling of being in touch" corresponds to the reality of being touched by the divine. The God whose presence is felt is a God who is confessed to be real.

We also saw in chapter 4 that people in psychedelic clinical trials often report that their drug session was one of the most meaningful experiences of their lives. Whether the experience of meaningfulness during a drug session strikes people as somehow in conflict with a general cultural sense of meaninglessness is a question that was posed but not entirely answered. Some claim that a sense of meaninglessness is especially strong today, partly explaining increases in the numbers of people who are seeking help for depression or anxiety.

A sense of the meaninglessness of it all is as old as the time of the first Greek philosophers. It was a common starting point for modern existentialists. Often, of course, the label "meaning-less" is used not philosophically but experientially. Whether or not the universe as a whole is meaningless is beside the point for many people who believe their job is meaningless, their relationships lack significance, and that no one will miss them when they are gone. Some use the word "meaningless" in this way to refer to church services or to the practices of the Christian faith. The theologians who reject the idea of experience as important to the Christian life seem to come close to saying that, experientially at least, Christianity really is meaningless.

By contrast, people claim that psychedelic drug sessions are profoundly meaningful. They seem to imply that this is a good thing, as if it goes without saying that meaningfulness is a thing to be valued in its contrast with the ordinary. It is not exactly clear what is meant by the sense of "meaningfulness" or why it seems to apply to psychedelic experiences. Is it something about the drug-brain-body interaction of the experience itself that makes it meaningful? Is it the subjective intensity at its peak? Or is it a compelling sense of significance that comes after the peak? Whatever it may be, the sense of the meaningfulness of the experience itself does not seem to fade over time.

Saying that a spiritual experience is meaningful is not the same as saying that a life is meaningful. In Christianity, in fact, there is a kind of inverse relationship between the two. An experience is meaningful precisely because of the sense of the numinous, which is the feeling of being in the presence of holy mystery. When that happens, the natural world takes on a new beauty and grandeur. Relationships are given new depths of empathy and joy. Everything that surrounds us is made glorious—everything, that is, except the self, which recedes more or less from view. The ego's defining boundaries are lowered, and its egocentrism dissolves as it enters a new feeling of unity with all that surrounds it.

Some Christian mystics went so far as to refer to self-loss as an annihilation of the self. Taken literally, their words became a problem because Christianity does not reject the goodness of created beings, even selfish ones. At the same time, Christianity agrees that self-centeredness is rejected. The ego is not the defining center of all reality and meaning. We find meaning when we are re-centered on something bigger than ourselves, in whose orbit we find purpose in a cause that outlives us, relationships that extend beyond us, and goals greater than anything we can achieve. A profound spiritual experience is meaningful because it cures us of trying to create our own meaning. A meaningful life is the gift that flows from a meaningful encounter.

A spiritual experience is an individual event, something that happens to one person even when surrounded by others who are sharing their own version of the experience. This is especially true of psychedelic experiences, and nearly all the research in psychedelic science is based on the human individual as the unit of study. The problem that this presents is that it can be misconstrued in a way that reinforces individualism. A psychedelic spiritual experience can make one feel a new level of connection with others and a diminished sense of self-importance, but the fact that it happens as an individual experience runs counter to the tendencies embedded in the experience itself. When the feeling of connectedness is felt when one is all alone, there is a risk that it will be interpreted not just as profoundly personal but as individualistic and individual-izing. Precisely because of their subjective intensity, psychedelic experiences may separate us from each other.

In Christian theology, however, what is personal is inherently communal, not individualistic. Theology rejects the modern idea of the isolated individual as the definition of personhood, drawing instead on its own ancient tradition that views the very meaning of the personal as existence in relationship. How will this play out for people who want to interpret their psychedelic spiritual expe-riences as compatible with their Christian faith? It is not simply that Christianity stresses the importance of the human commu-nity, something that science shows to be healthy. More than the pragmatic benefits of human contact are at stake for Christianity, which grounds its central doctrines in the idea of the social. The idea of the church as the context of salvation is perhaps the most obvious example. The idea of God as triune is also rooted in the notion that to be a person, human or divine, is to be defined by relationships to other persons. The social constitutes and defines the personal. One challenge Christianity faces in every age, most especially today, is how to bear witness to the reality of the social as greater than the reality of the individual.

In chapter 4, we looked at some of the debate over the ways in which psychedelic sessions seem to alter metaphysical beliefs. Individualism is just one of the ideas that might be challenged by psychedelic spiritual experiences. When we think about Christianity and metaphysics, it is fair to say that some meta-physical positions seem to be incompatible with Christianity, while some fit better than others. No philosophy or metaphysical theory can claim to be Christian to the exclusion of other theories. Some theologians drew heavily on Plato, others on Aristotle, still others on Kant, Hegel, or Whitehead. What are we to think, then, when we learn that psychedelic sessions can disrupt our theories and alter our beliefs? Should we worry that these experiences will undermine Christian belief? Should we wonder if they will undermine materialistic views and open the door to belief?

Anyone who thinks that Christianity is a closed and settled system of doctrines might be concerned. Christians who take drugs may have their beliefs rattled, and so some will think they should do everything they can to prevent the use of psychedelics. During the decades of the eighties and nineties, it seems that church leaders found this view compelling.

Should we be worried when we learn that spiritual experiences expand the consciousness and stretch the boundaries of what is possible? If psychedelics can bring about spiritual experiences, then we should expect that those who take these drugs might come away thinking that their metaphysical ideas about the nature of reality are changed. The evidence from scientific research suggests that alterations of metaphysical ideas will tilt people toward faith, not away from it. Some might see this as reassuring. Nothing, however, suggests that drugs will cause people to believe specific Christian doctrines.

In fact, psychedelic experiences might tilt them toward belief but lessen their confidence in specific beliefs. There is a tilt toward open-mindedness regarding past beliefs, not toward the embrace of new dogmas. Riskiness cannot be avoided any time something as foundational as metaphysical beliefs are altered. Whether this is something to welcome or fear may hinge on our theological understanding of grace, and in fact our ideas about grace might very well be the first metaphysical belief to be altered.

Does the feeling of the numinous lead to a belief in the gracious? If so, then the greatest of all the new ideas that may arise in the wake of a profound spiritual experience is that the experience itself is an encounter with grace. The metaphysical correlate of that awakening is that such a thing as grace truly exists and may be encountered. To interpret a spiritual experience as an encounter with grace is to give it a Christian interpretation. It is not that Christians have a monopoly on the idea of grace, but one cannot be a Christian without an openness to the abundance of grace. People with psychedelic spiritual experiences who want to interpret their experience as consistent with their Christian faith can begin by naming the numinous presence felt in their experience as the grace of a loving God.

ENCOUNTERS WITH GRACE

The numinous presence, of course, can be felt but left unnamed, although it seems that most people are open to the idea that what they encounter can be called "God" or something vaguely similar. The survey from the Pew Research Center confirms that even among the "nones," spiritual experiences occur for about a third of the population. They do not identify with religious institutions, and they keep their distance from many traditional doctrines. Avoiding religious institutions and doctrines, however, is not the same thing as rejecting belief in a divine reality. "Just 29% reject the notion that there is any higher power or spiritual force in the universe."[16] The rest of them are open to the idea that their spiritual experiences may have something to do with a transcendent spiritual reality.

The idea that people outside the church can have valid spiritual experiences is recognized theologically by Karl Rahner, who speaks of a spiritual experience as "an experience which any Christian (and indeed any human being) can have and can seek."[17] Spiritual experiences are human events that can happen to any human being regardless of religious participation. In and of themselves, the experiences are not tagged or labelled as Christian, as if the experiences possessed their own inherent properties that marked them uniquely and definitively as Christian experiences. What makes them spiritual in the first place is that people feel they are justified in calling them spiritual. They can take an added step, calling them not just spiritual but Christian, a label validated not by the form or features of the experience but by their decision to give it a Christian interpretation.

16. Pew, "Religious 'Nones' in America," 12.
17. Rahner, "Experience of the Holy Spirit," 193.

It is understandable that many today feel that they must decide against Christianity. They have good reasons for thinking that the church is a rigid institution that rejects spiritual experiences, especially if those experiences have anything to do with psychedelics. Our task at this point is to try to say why this need not be so. Christianity can and should be open to every form or variation of spiritual experience, including experiences that occur with the use of psychedelic drugs. Persuading Christians that this is true is just the first step. Persuading psychedelic users that Christians are open to their experience is a second step that can only be taken if the first step is successful.

Those with psychedelic spiritual experiences may actively resist the idea of a Christian interpretation, seeing it as intrusive or coercive. They may be suspicious of offers from Christians to support the process of interpretation, fearing that support is subterfuge for proselytizing. They know that traditional Christianity has no place in its teachings for psychedelics. More than that, they may have felt rejected by Christians or churches, especially if they suffer from mental illness and have turned to psychedelic-assisted therapy. Perhaps they are troubled by church scandals of recent decades or count themselves among the victims of spiritual abuse, made to feel shame or hatred because of their identity or preyed upon by officials. People today can take their pick among the reasons for staying away from the church.

Resistance is also likely to come from those who identify with traditional Christianity. They might ask where psychedelics are mentioned in the Bible. They are not likely to be persuaded by views of scholars who claim that the scriptures contain hints here and there that imply the use of psychedelics. It is generally accepted that the ancient mystery cults, especially the long-running Eleusinian Mysteries, involved some sort of secret drugs, and Christianity grew alongside these cults before finally shutting them down. Brian Muraresku argues that the use of mind-altering substances is present from the beginning of Christianity.[18] His arguments are interesting and thought-provoking, but they are

18. Muraresku, *Immortality Key*.

unlikely to shake the confidence of conservative Catholic or Protestant believers in more standard interpretations of the Bible.

Objections notwithstanding, how might someone go about interpreting a meaningful spiritual experience with psychedelics as compatible with Christian faith? We have already pointed to the central role that the idea of grace will play in their interpretation. This is true whenever we speak in Christian terms about spiritual experiences, not just when psychedelics are involved. According to Michael Sells, grace is essential to Christian mysticism. "A mysticism that leaves out the element of grace by focusing exclusively on the realization of a purely natural potential, or one that makes a separation between those who are able to achieve mystical knowledge and those who are not, will run counter to guiding theological concerns."[19] This point is especially urgent when it comes to psychedelics. It is not the natural potential of the person or the natural effects of the drugs that account theologically for what is happening in a profound and numinous experience. Grace is the explanation for a gracious encounter.

In Christian theology, grace is so closely connected with the Holy Spirit that the two are sometimes spoken of interchangeably, as if grace is the Spirit and the Spirit is grace. To say that any Christian view of mystical experience must be grounded on a doctrine of grace is therefore to say that it is the work of the Holy Spirit. Pneumatology, the doctrine of the Spirit, is the theological foundation for spiritual experience. Here again, Zahl is helpful in his clarity when he says that when we are "speaking about 'experience' in Christian theology we are speaking at the same time about the doctrine of the Holy Spirit. . . . Above all, the theological topic of Christian 'experience' is deeply and necessarily intertwined with the theology of the Holy Spirit, such that it is not really possible to speak persuasively or rigorously about the place and function of 'experience' in Christian theology apart from the theological framework of pneumatology."[20] The encounter with grace is an encounter with the Holy Spirit. "Christian theology . . . holds that

19. Sells, "From a History," 396.
20. Zahl, *Holy Spirit*, 3.

experience of God is to be understood and described first and foremost as experience of God the Holy Spirit."[21]

What this means for Christian theology broadly is that the grace of the Spirit who encounters some is accessible to all. Rahner is right when he claims that "Christianity . . . is not elitist."[22] When it is true to itself, Christianity understands that what is given to one is available to all, equally and in full measure. This is true for those outside Christianity, and it is true for those whose experiences involve the use of psychedelics.

In personal terms, this means several things at once. First, it provides a kind of reassurance that the experience, whatever its own strengths or limitations might be, does not depend on the person who has it. If the Holy Spirit is the active agent making possible the gracious encounter at the center of the spiritual experience, then there is a certain degree of passivity on the part of the person having the experience. William James claimed that passivity is one of the marks of mystical experiences, not to suggest that people were unaware of what was happening but that they were experiencing it as something that happened to them, not as something that they caused to happen. According to James, mystics feel as if their "own will were in abeyance, and indeed sometimes as if . . . [they] were grasped and held by a superior power."[23]

Second, it suggests that there is a theological basis for trusting the content and the direction of the experience, even a psychedelic experience. There are risks involved, starting with the very real possibility that the experience will be difficult. Another risk is that it is likely to unsettle old ideas and beliefs. In chapter 4, we saw how psychedelic experiences can alter fundamental beliefs. One explanation offered for metaphysical unsettling was based in the REBUS theory, which brings together neuroscientific tools with subjective descriptions to suggest that intense psychedelic experience can free the mind from its reliance on its former beliefs. Freedom from negative thinking might have the effect of treating

21. Zahl, *Holy Spirit*, 52.

22. Rahner, "Experience of the Holy Spirit," 207.

23. James, *Varieties of Religious Experience*, 210.

our mental disorders. But what about freedom from our religious or theological ideas, especially negative religious ideas wrapped up in themes of judgment, shame, and failure? How can one trust the disruptive effects of spiritual experiences, especially when psychedelics are involved?

Theology is never in a position to say to someone that we know that what happened to them in their experience is the work of the Holy Spirit, implying that they should just go with the experience and trust it without examining it. The person with the experience can choose to be open to the possibility that what is encountered is the Spirit. Openness turns next to testing it out in terms of its staying power and its practical consequences. Here is where the idea of experience as a process is theologically important and the ideas offered by David Lamberth can be so helpful. What Christianity offers is an invitation, not a guarantee. To those who have an intense or surprising spiritual experience, it invites them to walk with the process of experience to its end, with all its twists and turns, always wondering, and always open to the next surprise. Hold the moment of intensity with affection, and do not be afraid to ask where it is going.

According to Bernard McGinn, "Christian mystical theology is based upon the twin premises of the unknowability of God on the one hand and God's accessibility to love on the other."[24] Over and over again in the Christian mystical tradition, if God is described at all, it is as an incomprehensible mystery. The more mystical the theologian, the greater the reticence in trying to describe God or list the divine attributes. From Gregory of Nyssa to Karl Rahner, the most mystical among Christian theologians tend to describe God as inaccessible and incomprehensible mystery. What the spiritual experience offers is the conviction that the holy mystery is accessible, present, and lovable. It offers a relation, not information.

The closer we are, the greater the mystery. A spiritual awakening is not a gift of knowledge about God. Much more than that, it is a growing confidence in God's presence, in being loved, and in becoming more loving. It is to experience what scripture might be

24. McGinn, "Love, Knowledge," 12.

describing when it tells us of the "Spirit bearing witness with our spirit that we are children of God" (Rom 8:16). The text is clear that the witness of the encountering Spirit is to assure us that we are in a relationship with the holy. The relationship, the presence, and the sense of the numinous far outstrip the conceptual or doctrinal.

Despite the fact that Rahner was an expert in the doctrines of the church, he writes that a person's "decision of faith" does not come from doctrines or any sort of "pedagogic indoctrination." It comes instead "from the experience of God . . . bursting out of the very heart of human existence and able to be really experienced."[25]

What is this experience that bursts out of the very heart of our lives? Is it not an encounter with grace in abundance? Old ideas are dislodged as new possibilities take their place. A sense of spiritual awe spreads itself until if fills every moment. Over it all is a feeling of discovery of newness everywhere. A new creation, a newly revised life story, a new hopefulness, all from an encounter with a love that makes all things new.

25. Rahner, "Spirituality," 148.

7

A Spiritual Home for
Psychedelics Seekers

EVERYTHING WE HAVE COVERED so far in this book leads us to think that soon, people who have psychedelic spiritual experiences will turn to the church to find community and support. Some have already made their move. Some of them, in fact, have become seminary students or are serving in positions of church leadership. They may decide it is best to keep quiet about their experiences. Others might mention it as a part of their past life before they came to faith. A few might describe how their experiences awakened within them a hunger for human spiritual companionship and for a connection with a faith tradition with deep historic roots.

Their pathway to the church might be through a casual use of psychedelics, perhaps with little or no preparation and support but with just enough spiritual intensity in their experience to get them wondering. Or their experience may have been with the help of a skilled but underground guide, part of a journey taken by themselves or with others in a small group. Some will have their experience on a retreat, possibly one involving international travel to one of the few countries that allows access to drugs like psilocybin.

In a few years, assuming that proposals for psychedelic-assisted therapy are approved as expected, the most common psychedelic pathway to the church will hinge on a spiritual experience in the context of therapy. Part of each person's story might include a history of dealing with mental health challenges, such as PTSD, depression, or substance abuse. What they discovered is that their drug session in the context of therapy awakened a new level of awareness. As they explored the significance of their experience in the context of the process of integration, it became clear that they were searching for contact with a spiritual community. After thinking about it for a while, perhaps they will call a pastor or visit a church. If so, how will they be received? Will they dare to speak of what has happened to them? Will they sense that if they talk about what is really going on, they will be rejected?

FROM CONDEMNATION TO INVITATION

Christian churches today do not have nearly the level of cultural influence that they had half a century ago, and most regard that as a good thing. Our collective influence, however, has not disappeared entirely, especially on questions of health and human flourishing. How we should use our voice in public has never been a matter of agreement among the various Christian traditions. What to say is even less clear, and sometimes various denominations have spoken publicly against the public witness of other churches. Different views on how to address the challenge of psychedelic spirituality might translate into competing public statements.

Not that the official opinions of the churches matter very much when it comes to biomedical research involving psychedelics or to the regulatory approval processes already underway. No one is asking the church to bless psychedelic-assisted therapy, nor should they. Churches may play a small role on questions of decriminalization. When the public is asked to vote, a few voters might wonder what their church has to say before they make up their minds.

Churches have spoken about psychedelics, but their official guidance is limited to a few terse comments that seem largely stuck in 1980s and '90s. The United Methodist Church, the second largest

Protestant denomination in the US, condemns psychedelic drugs in its official policy manual, the *Book of Resolutions*. "Psychedelics or hallucinogens, which include LSD, psilocybin, mescaline, PCP, and DMT, produce changes in perception and altered states of consciousness. Not only is medical use of psychedelics or hallucinogens limited, if present at all, but the use of these drugs may result in permanent psychiatric problems."[1]

The Presbyterian Church (USA) makes a point of condemning the racially unjust mass incarceration triggered by the war on drugs. At the same time, Presbyterians warn about the dangers of these drugs. "Psychoactive drugs can mask emotional pain, preventing us from squarely facing the truth of our lives. They can distract and demotivate. They can promise the rewards of pleasure without summoning achievement or transformation. This, coupled with the human propensity to self-deception, is what makes some drugs so attractive, insidious, and disorienting."[2] Judged in the light of recent research, these comments are so far off the mark that they can be dismissed as simply untrue. Keeping them in place is an embarrassment to the churches and an obstacle standing in the way of the role they are called to play.

Catholic statements also condemn the use of psychedelics unless there is a clear therapeutic intention.[3] According to the Roman Catholic catechism, "*The use of drugs* inflicts very grave damage on human health and life. Their use, except on strictly therapeutic grounds, is a grave offense."[4] Thanks to biomedical research, evidence of therapeutic benefit is well established and growing by the day. If Catholics are permitted to use these drugs for therapy, it seems that the moral traffic light is about to turn from red to green. It will be interesting to see if Catholic leaders update their guidance in response to the development of psychedelic-assisted therapy. An even more interesting question

1. United Methodist Church, "Alcohol and Other Drugs," 164.

2. Presbyterian Church (USA), "Putting Healing Before Punishment," 14.

3. McCarthy, "Christianity and Psychedelic Medicine."

4. Catholic Church, "Respect for the Dignity," para. 2291; emphasis original.

for Catholics is whether a therapeutic intention requires use of a licensed therapy center. Using online surveys, researchers are finding that many people use these drugs outside formal channels for mental health purposes, perhaps because of cost but more likely because of legal hurdles. They do so with a clear therapeutic intention. Will that count for Catholics?

Imagine for a moment that one or more of the major denominations decided to create a new public statement on psychedelics. What would it say? It would begin by pointing out the theological foundations in scripture and tradition that highlight the importance of human experiences of encounters with the divine, noting the variety of forms these experiences can take. Critically and carefully, it would review current research, note the solid evidence of real health benefits, and commend the work of scientists. It would offer support and approval to any serious effort to offer psychedelic-assisted therapy, noting of course its concerns for availability, affordability, social justice, and the safety of vulnerable patients.

A church statement would say a lot about so-called challenging or difficult psychedelic experiences, noting their psychiatric and spiritual dimensions. It would avoid hype, call attention to the numbers of people involved, and lament the failures of the war on drugs. It would pledge to support indigenous peoples and their traditions that use psychedelics, such as the Native American Church and Sante Daimo, and offer to cooperate wherever possible with new "plant-sacrament" churches, defending equal protections under the Religious Freedom Restoration Act for all sincere spiritual seekers. Above all, it would encourage and bless all those who, through their use of psychedelic drugs in any context, have come to a new spiritual awareness, regardless of their religious beliefs. It would encourage local congregations and leaders to extend a welcome to all who are seeking the presence of the Spirit, asking each church to pledge to be a safe place.

Churches and their leaders should understand that there is no way to dodge these issues. If millions of people come through some version of psychedelic-assisted therapy, and some proportion of them (half, at least) have a spiritual experience as a result, and some fraction of these have questions for pastors and church leaders, what response will they receive? What will we say to those who turn to the church as a spiritual home in which they can talk safely and honestly about their experiences with psychedelic drugs? Saying nothing is not an option. Our old statements still speak, and our support of the war on drugs still functions as our default position. Saying nothing new amounts to what Karl Rahner warns about when he speaks of "our culpable lack of creative imagination and boldness of spirit." What we need, he says, is "a sharper ear, a keener eye, a livelier anticipation to the slightest indication that somewhere that Spirit is stirring."[5]

SPIRITUAL SUPPORT FOR PSYCHEDELIC SEEKERS

When it comes to the future of psychedelic spirituality, is it possible for churches and their leaders to move from condemnation to invitation? For that to happen, churches will have to change, led perhaps in response to the boldness of a few leaders here and there. To be effective, however, the public's perception of churches will need to change as well. This may not happen easily. Based on reports like the 2024 study from the Pew Research Center, there are millions of people who see themselves as spiritual and who claim to have spiritual experiences, but who avoid religious affiliation because of bad experiences with churches and with Christians. Even if churches really became places of welcome for unaffiliated spiritual seekers, including psychedelic spiritual seekers, how many of them would trust the church to be a safe spiritual home?

At a deeper level, the problem here is not merely the public perception of the church, nor is it limited to the way church people tend to view psychedelics. Spirituality in any form is not exactly at home in the church. In many Christian settings, spiritual experiences are not fostered and not exactly welcomed. In academic theology, experience has been questioned, marginalized, and

---

5. Rahner, "Do Not Stifle the Spirit!" 80–81.

dismissed as a source for Christian insight. Generations of seminarians have been taught that the experiential is not to be trusted, much less valued or lifted up in Christian communities. There are signs of renewal, but there is still a long way to go. The phenomenon of psychedelic spiritual experiences merely compounds the problem by giving traditional gatekeepers another reason to exclude the spiritual and experiential.

Whenever it ignores or denigrates the significance of spiritual experience, theology itself can be an obstacle that stands in the way of all spiritual seekers, not just those whose experiences are connected to psychedelics. Theological leaders like Karl Rahner have called on the church to welcome the mystic and the seeker. The church needs the mystic and the spiritual seeker for its very survival. According to Rahner, "The Christian of the future will be a mystic or [they] will not exist at all." Watching the emptying of the churches in late twentieth century Europe, it is as if Rahner is envisioning a time when there might still be a few Christians left, but no church of any note. The few Christians who remain, he says, will be mystics and seekers. In the very next sentences, however, it is as if Rahner is warning us today to guard ourselves against the fantasy that by themselves psychedelics or any other momentary spiritual experience can help. By mysticism, he means more than intense subjective experience, and his claim that the Christian of the future must be a mystic presupposes a deeper meaning on his part. "If by mysticism we mean, not singular parapsychological phenomena, but a genuine experience of God emerging from the very heart of our existence, this statement is very true and its truth and importance will become still clearer in the spirituality of the future."[6]

Another writer highly valued for his writings on spirituality is Thomas Merton (1915–68), who also warned about the emptiness of Christianity without mysticism. In a set of lectures given to novices at his monastery in the 1960s, Merton began with this challenge:

6. Rahner, "Spirituality," 148.

Without mysticism there is no real theology, and without theology there is no real mysticism. Hence the emphasis will be on mysticism as theology, to bring out clearly the mystical dimensions of our theology, hence to help us to do what we must really do: live our theology. Some think it is sufficient to come to the monastery to live the rule. More is required—we must live our theology, fully, deeply, in its totality. Without this, there is no sanctity. The separation of theology from "spirituality" is a disaster.[7]

If the separation of theology from spirituality was a disaster in the early sixties when the church was at the peak of its influence, how much more so is this true now that the church is declining in almost every way.

To ask for the church of today to become a place that welcomes psychedelic spiritual seekers requires first of all that it becomes a place that welcomes and encourages all forms and pathways to spiritual experience. Psychedelics aside, many churches are not attentive to the spiritual needs or the spiritual experiences of their members. "Do not stifle the Spirit," Rahner warns, taking the text of 1 Thessalonians 5:19 as the title of an essay. The biblical injunction is not merely "an obvious and universal principle, but of an urgent imperative precisely for us in the here and now."[8] He was worried that the church would push away all those who encountered the divine, stifling the Spirit by shunning the spiritual. The church has always had self-isolating saints who were known to hide from human contact in caves or deserts. In contrast to spirituality in isolation, Rahner commends the benefits of "community as a real and essential element of the spirituality of tomorrow."[9] When it welcomes spiritual seekers with the benefits of community, the community itself will be the greatest beneficiary.

It is not likely that the church as a whole will soon become a place of welcome for psychedelic spiritual seekers. Christianity has never been monolithic, however, and local congregations

7. Merton, *Course in Christian Mysticism*, 1.

8. Rahner, "Do Not Stifle the Spirit!" 77.

9. Rahner, "Spirituality," 150.

here or there might move in this direction while others wait. Some of these may even be successful in getting the message out in their local area that they are a place that welcomes all spiritual seekers. Their message is a simple offer of nonjudgmental spiritual companionship, a pledge of safety and confidentiality, and most of all a promise to receive as holy gifts the experiences of the Spirit, regardless of their human context.

Should the invitation be accepted? Individual seekers can only answer for themselves. Past experiences with Christianity might be wholly negative, and so their answer is to avoid contact at all costs. A few might tap into a mix of memories that includes a fond sense of connection with others. Some might accept the invitation because doing so is suggested by secular or medical sources, thinking it must be safe if scientists recommend it. The Multidisciplinary Association for Psychedelic Studies (MAPS) has released an online handbook to guide people through the psychedelic integration process. Noting that the various dimensions of human experience include the spiritual, the handbook offers this advice: "Regardless of your specific beliefs (or lack thereof), we encourage you to consciously and intentionally explore how your experiences relate to the domain of Spirit during your periods of integration."[10] This can be done alone, of course, or with the help of an individual guide or spiritual director. But it also can be done in community and with the goal of trying to unpack the meaning of a psychedelic spiritual experience within the context of a Christian community and a Christian view of life.

Anyone following the advice in the handbook can reach out to various sources of support. Among them are institutional chaplains, local underground networks, plant-sacrament churches, and pastors who are ready to provide the care that is needed. A teamwork approach can be best so that the limitations of each person can be offset. Local church leaders or pastors, however, can play a special role, especially when they have the benefit of a long-term relationship with the spiritual seeker. They are also in a

10. Multidisciplinary Association for Psychedelic Studies, "MAPS Psychedelic Integration Workbook."

unique position to influence the thinking of the wider congregation, reminding people publicly that the gift of communal spiritual support is one of the main reasons for the congregation's existence.

To do all this, church leaders need just the right mix of caution and courage. Psychedelics are powerful substances. They are illegal almost everywhere. Despite steps toward decriminalization, drug seizures are increasing, not decreasing. Difficult or challenging experiences can happen, and they can be frightening. We all should respect the vulnerability and the suggestibility of those who have just engaged in a psychedelic experience.

Courage is also needed. Once again, the words of Karl Rahner are most helpful. He asks us to have "the courage to take risks." The very idea that psychedelic spiritual experiences can be interpreted as part of a Christian life is an idea that requires boldness, what Rahner calls "the utmost extremes of boldness in our attitude towards the new and the untried." To those who prefer a way that is safer, he tells us that "the surest way is the boldest." Our moment calls for "the utmost boldness in taking risks."[11]

For churches today, the boldest step of all is to recognize that a psychedelic spiritual experience can be a true and transformative encounter with the grace of God.

11. Rahner, "Do Not Stifle the Spirit!" 81.

Bibliography

Aaronson, Scott T., et al. "Single-Dose Synthetic Psilocybin with Psychotherapy for Treatment-Resistant Bipolar Type II Major Depressive Episodes: A Nonrandomized Controlled Trial." *JAMA Psychiatry* 81 (2024) 555–62. https://doi.org/10.1001/jamapsychiatry.2023.4685.

American Psychiatric Association. *Diagnostic and Statistical Manual of Mental Disorders.* 5th ed. Washington, DC: American Psychiatric Association, 2013.

Arnaud, Kevin O., St., and Donald Sharpe. "Entheogens and Spiritual Seeking: The Quest for Self-Transcendence, Psychological Well-Being, and Psychospiritual Growth." *Journal of Psychedelic Studies* 7.1 (April 21, 2023) 69–79. https://doi.org/10.1556/2054.2023.00263.

Barrett, Frederick S., et al. "The Challenging Experience Questionnaire: Characterization of Challenging Experiences with Psilocybin Mushrooms." *Journal of Psychopharmacology* 30.12 (December 1, 2016) 1279–95. https://doi.org/10.1177/0269881116678781.

Beans, Carolyn. "If Psychedelics Heal, How Do They Do It?" *Proceedings of the National Academy of Sciences* 121.2 (January 9, 2024) 1–6. https://doi.org/10.1073/pnas.2321906121.

Bogenschutz, Michael P., et al. "Percentage of Heavy Drinking Days Following Psilocybin-Assisted Psychotherapy vs Placebo in the Treatment of Adult Patients With Alcohol Use Disorder: A Randomized Clinical Trial." *JAMA Psychiatry* 79.10 (October 1, 2022) 953–62. https://doi.org/10.1001/jamapsychiatry.2022.2096.

Bosch, Oliver G., et al. "Psychedelics in the Treatment of Unipolar and Bipolar Depression." *International Journal of Bipolar Disorders* 10.1 (July 5, 2022) 1–16. https://doi.org/10.1186/s40345-022-00265-5.

Brett, Jonathan, et al. "Exploring Psilocybin-Assisted Psychotherapy in the Treatment of Methamphetamine Use Disorder." *Frontiers in Psychiatry* 14 (2023) 1–7. https://www.frontiersin.org/articles/10.3389/fpsyt.2023.1123424.

Carhart-Harris, R. L., and K. J. Friston. "REBUS and the Anarchic Brain: Toward a Unified Model of the Brain Action of Psychedelics." *Pharmacological Reviews* 71.3 (July 1, 2019) 316–44. https://doi.org/10.1124/pr.118.017160.

Carhart-Harris, Robin, et al. "The Entropic Brain: A Theory of Conscious States Informed by Neuroimaging Research with Psychedelic Drugs." *Frontiers in Human Neuroscience* 8 (2014) 1–22. https://www.frontiersin.org/articles/10.3389/fnhum.2014.00020.

Carhart-Harris, R. L., et al. "LSD Enhances Suggestibility in Healthy Volunteers." *Psychopharmacology* 232.4 (February 2015) 785–94. https://doi.org/10.1007/s00213-014-3714-z.

Carr, Anne. "Theology and Experience in the Thought of Karl Rahner." *The Journal of Religion* 53.3 (July 1973) 359–76. https://doi.org/10.1086/486351.

Catholic Church. "Respect for the Dignity of Persons." In *Catechism of the Catholic Church: Revised in Accordance with the Official Latin Text Promulgated by Pope John Paul II*, para. 2291. Washington, DC: United States Catholic Conference. 2000.

Cherian, Kirsten N., et al. "Magnesium-Ibogaine Therapy in Veterans with Traumatic Brain Injuries." *Nature Medicine* (January 5, 2024) 373–81. https://doi.org/10.1038/s41591-023-02705-w.

Ching, Terence H. W., et al. "Safety, Tolerability, and Clinical and Neural Effects of Single-Dose Psilocybin in Obsessive-Compulsive Disorder: Protocol for a Randomized, Double-Blind, Placebo-Controlled, Non-Crossover Trial." *Frontiers in Psychiatry* 14 (2023) 1–12. https://www.frontiersin.org/articles/10.3389/fpsyt.2023.1178529.

Cole-Turner, Ron. "Psychedelic Epistemology: William James and the 'Noetic Quality' of Mystical Experience." *Religions* 12.12 (December 2021) 1–16. https://doi.org/10.3390/rel12121058.

———. "Psychedelic Mysticism and Christian Spirituality: From Science to Love." *Religions* 15.5 (May 2024) 537. https://doi.org/10.3390/rel15050537.

Davis, Alan K., et al. "Effects of Psilocybin-Assisted Therapy on Major Depressive Disorder: A Randomized Clinical Trial." *JAMA Psychiatry* 78.5 (May 1, 2021) 481–89. https://doi.org/10.1001/jamapsychiatry.2020.3285.

Davis, Alan K., et al. "Increases in Psychological Flexibility Mediate Relationship Between Acute Psychedelic Effects and Decreases in Racial Trauma Symptoms Among People of Color." *Chronic Stress* 5 (January 1, 2021) 1–10. https://doi.org/10.1177/24705470211035607.

Davis, Alan K., et al. "Survey of Entity Encounter Experiences Occasioned by Inhaled N,N-Dimethyltryptamine: Phenomenology, Interpretation, and Enduring Effects." *Journal of Psychopharmacology* 34.9 (September 1, 2020) 1008–20. https://doi.org/10.1177/0269881120916143.

Del Colle, Ralph. "John Wesley's Doctrine of Grace in Light of the Christian Tradition." *International Journal of Systematic Theology* 4.2 (July 2002) 172–89. https://doi.org/10.1111/1463-1652.00079.

Doblin, Rick. "Pahnke's 'Good Friday Experiment': A Long-Term Follow-up and Methodological Critique." *Journal of Transpersonal Psychology* 23.1 (1991) 1–28.

Dupré, Louis. "The Christian Experience of Mystical Union." *The Journal of Religion* 69.1 (1989) 1–13.

Eisenstein, Michael. "The Psychedelic Escape from Depression." *Nature* 609 (September 28, 2022) S87–89. https://doi.org/10.1038/d41586-022-02872-9.

Esser, Marissa B., et al. "Estimated Deaths Attributable to Excessive Alcohol Use among US Adults Aged 20 to 64 Years, 2015 to 2019." *JAMA Network Open* 5.11 (November 1, 2022) 1–8. https://doi.org/10.1001/jamanetworkopen.2022.39485.

Evans, Jules, et al. "Extended Difficulties Following the Use of Psychedelic Drugs: A Mixed Methods Study." *PLOS ONE* 18.10 (October 24, 2023) 1–24. https://doi.org/10.1371/journal.pone.0293349.

Frymann, Tomas, et al. "The Psychedelic Integration Scales: Tools for Measuring Psychedelic Integration Behaviors and Experiences." *Frontiers in Psychology* 13 (2022) 1–20. https://www.frontiersin.org/articles/10.3389/fpsyg.2022.863247.

Garcia-Romeu, Albert, et al. "Psychedelics as Novel Therapeutics in Alzheimer's Disease: Rationale and Potential Mechanisms." In *Disruptive Psychopharmacology*, edited by Frederick S. Barrett and Katrin H. Preller, 287–317. Current Topics in Behavioral Neurosciences. Cham: Springer, 2022. https://doi.org/10.1007/7854_2021_267.

Gładziejewski, Paweł. "From Altered States to Metaphysics: The Epistemic Status of Psychedelic-Induced Metaphysical Beliefs." *Review of Philosophy and Psychology* (October 10, 2023) 1–23. https://doi.org/10.1007/s13164-023-00709-6.

Griffiths, Roland R., et al. "Psilocybin Can Occasion Mystical-Type Experiences Having Substantial and Sustained Personal Meaning and Spiritual Significance." *Psychopharmacology* 187.3 (2006) 268–83.

Griffiths, Roland R., et al. "Survey of Subjective 'God Encounter Experiences': Comparisons among Naturally Occurring Experiences and Those Occasioned by the Classic Psychedelics Psilocybin, LSD, Ayahuasca, or DMT." *PLOS ONE* 14.4 (April 23, 2019) 1–26. https://doi.org/10.1371/journal.pone.0214377.

Grob, Charles S., and Gary Bravo. "The High Road: History and Hysteria." In *Higher Wisdom: Eminent Elders Explore the Continuing Impact of Psychedelics*, edited by Roger Walsh and Charles S. Grob, 7–18. New York: SUNY Press, 2005. https://doi.org/10.1515/9780791482964-003.

Gukasyan, Natalie, et al. "Efficacy and Safety of Psilocybin-Assisted Treatment for Major Depressive Disorder: Prospective 12-Month Follow-Up." *Journal of Psychopharmacology* 36.2 (February 1, 2022) 151–58. https://doi.org/10.1177/02698811211073759.

Hartogsohn, Ido. "The Meaning-Enhancing Properties of Psychedelics and Their Mediator Role in Psychedelic Therapy, Spirituality, and Creativity." *Frontiers in Neuroscience* 12 (2018) 1–5. https://doi.org/10.3389/fnins.2018.00129.

Hipólito, Inês, et al. "Pattern Breaking: A Complex Systems Approach to Psychedelic Medicine." *Neuroscience of Consciousness* 1 (January 1, 2023) 1–16. https://doi.org/10.1093/nc/niad017.

Husain, Muhammad Ishrat, et al. "Psilocybin for Treatment-Resistant Depression without Psychedelic Effects: Study Protocol for a 4-Week, Double-Blind, Proof-of-Concept Randomised Controlled Trial." *BJPsych Open* 9.4 (July 2023) 1–9. https://doi.org/10.1192/bjo.2023.535.

Huxley, Aldous. *The Doors of Perception.* New York: Harper, 1954.

James, William. *The Varieties of Religious Experience: A Study in Human Nature, Being the Gifford Lectures on Natural Religion Delivered at Edinburgh in 1901–1902.* New York: Dover, 2018.

Jantzen, Grace M. "Mysticism and Experience." *Religious Studies* 25.3 (September 1989) 295–315.

Johnson, Luke Timothy. *Religious Experience in Earliest Christianity: A Missing Dimension in New Testament Studies.* Minneapolis: Fortress, 1998.

Johnson, Matthew W., et al. "Classic Psychedelics: An Integrative Review of Epidemiology, Therapeutics, Mystical Experience, and Brain Network Function." *Pharmacology & Therapeutics* 197 (May 1, 2019) 83–102. https://doi.org/10.1016/j.pharmthera.2018.11.010.

Johnson, Matthew W., et al. "Long-Term Follow-up of Psilocybin-Facilitated Smoking Cessation." *The American Journal of Drug and Alcohol Abuse* 43.1 (January 2017) 55–60. https://doi.org/10.3109/00952990.2016.1170135.

Johnson, Matthew W., et al. "Pilot Study of the 5-HT2AR Agonist Psilocybin in the Treatment of Tobacco Addiction." *Journal of Psychopharmacology* 28.11 (November 2014) 983–92. https://doi.org/10.1177/0269881114548296.

Johnstad, Petter. "Entheogenic Spirituality: Characteristics of Spiritually Motivated Psychedelics Use." *The International Journal for the Psychology of Religion* 33.4 (October 2, 2023) 380–96. https://doi.org/10.1080/10508619.2022.2148060.

Jylkkä, Jussi, et al. "Endorsement of Metaphysical Idealism Mediates a Link Between Past Use of Psychedelics and Wellbeing." *PsyArXiv* (December 22, 2023) 1–24. doi:10.31234/osf.io/kazf2.

Kelly, John R., et al. "Psychedelic Therapy's Transdiagnostic Effects: A Research Domain Criteria (RDoC) Perspective." *Frontiers in Psychiatry* 12 (2021) 1–39. https://doi.org/10.3389/fpsyt.2021.800072.

Kočárová, Rita, et al. "Does Psychedelic Therapy Have a Transdiagnostic Action and Prophylactic Potential?" *Frontiers in Psychiatry* 12 (July 19, 2021) 1–18. https://doi.org/10.3389/fpsyt.2021.661233.

Labate, Beatriz Caiuby, and Clancy Cavnar, eds. *Psychedelic Justice: Toward a Diverse and Equitable Psychedelic Culture.* Santa Fe, NM: Synergetic, 2021.

Lamberth, David C. "Putting 'Experience' to the Test in Theological Reflection." *The Harvard Theological Review* 93.1 (2000) 67–77.

Lattin, Don. *God on Psychedelics: Tripping Across the Rubble of Old-Time Religion.* Berkeley, CA: Apocryphile, 2023.

Londoño, Ernesto. "After Six-Decade Hiatus, Experimental Psychedelic Therapy Returns to the V.A." *New York Times*, section A, page 14 of the New York ed., June 24, 2022. https://www.nytimes.com/2022/06/24/us/politics/psychedelic-therapy-veterans.html.

Macallan, Brian Claude. "Christian Responses to Psilocybin-Assisted Therapy and Potential Religious and Spiritual Experiences." *Religions* 14.10 (October 2023) 1–9. https://doi.org/10.3390/rel14101312.

MacDougall, Scott. "On the Theological Status of Experience in Seminary Formation." *Anglican Theological Review* 104.4 (November 2022) 426–35. https://doi.org/10.1177/00033286221126321.

MacLean KA, et al. "Mystical Experiences Occasioned by the Hallucinogen Psilocybin Lead to Increases in the Personality Domain of Openness." *Journal of Psychopharmacology* 11 (2011) 1453–61.

"Major Depression." National Institute of Mental Health, July 2023. https://www.nimh.nih.gov/health/statistics/major-depression.

Mans, Keri, et al. "Sustained, Multifaceted Improvements in Mental Well-Being Following Psychedelic Experiences in a Prospective Opportunity Sample." *Frontiers in Psychiatry* 12 (2021) 1–17. https://doi.org/10.3389/fpsyt.2021.647909.

Markopoulos, Athanasios, et al. "Evaluating the Potential Use of Serotonergic Psychedelics in Autism Spectrum Disorder." *Frontiers in Pharmacology* 12 (2021) 1–15. https://doi.org/10.3389/fphar.2021.749068.

McCarthy, Bryan. "Christianity and Psychedelic Medicine: A Pastoral Approach." *Christian Bioethics: Non-Ecumenical Studies in Medical Morality* 29.1 (March 1, 2023) 31–57. https://doi.org/10.1093/cb/cbac008.

McGinn, Bernard. "'Evil-Sounding, Rash, and Suspect of Heresy': Tensions between Mysticism and Magisterium in the History of the Church." *The Catholic Historical Review* 90.2 (2004) 193–212.

———. *The Foundations of Mysticism.* Vol 1, *The Presence of God: A History of Western Christian Mysticism.* New York: Crossroad, 1991.

———. "Love, Knowledge, and Mystical Union in Western Christianity: Twelfth to Sixteenth Centuries." *Church History* 56.1 (1987) 7–24. https://doi.org/10.2307/3165301.

———. "Mysticism and the Reformation: A Brief Survey." *Acta Theologica* 35.2 (2015) 50–65. https://doi.org/10.4314/actat.v35i2.4.

Meer, Pim B. van der, et al. "Therapeutic Effect of Psilocybin in Addiction: A Systematic Review." *Frontiers in Psychiatry* 14 (2023) 1–10. https://www.frontiersin.org/articles/10.3389/fpsyt.2023.1134454.

Merton, Thomas. *A Course in Christian Mysticism: Thirteen Sessions with the Famous Trappist Monk.* Edited by Jon M. Sweeney. Collegeville, MN: Liturgical, 2017.

Mitchell, Jennifer M., and Brian T. Anderson. "Psychedelic Therapies Reconsidered: Compounds, Clinical Indications, and Cautious Optimism." *Neuropsychopharmacology* (July 21, 2023) 96–103. https://doi.org/10.1038/s41386-023-01656-7.

Mitchell, Jennifer M., et al. "MDMA-Assisted Therapy for Severe PTSD: A Randomized, Double-Blind, Placebo-Controlled Phase 3 Study." *Nature Medicine* 27.6 (June 2021) 2473–80. https://doi.org/10.1038/s41591-021-01336-3.

Multidisciplinary Association for Psychedelic Studies. "The MAPS Psychedelic Integration Workbook." Multidisciplinary Association for Psychedelic Studies, n.d. https://maps.org/integration-station/.

Mundall, Ian. "Psychedelic Therapy May Help Break the Chains of Gambling Addiction." *Imperial News*, January 11, 2024. https://www.imperial.ac.uk/news/250473/psychedelic-therapy-help-break-chains-gambling/.

Muraresku, Brian C. *The Immortality Key: The Secret History of the Religion with No Name.* New York: St. Martin's, 2020.

Nayak, Sandeep M., et al. "Belief Changes Associated with Psychedelic Use." *Journal of Psychopharmacology* 37.1 (January 1, 2023) 80–92. https://doi.org/10.1177/02698811221131989.

Olson, David E. "The Subjective Effects of Psychedelics May Not Be Necessary for Their Enduring Therapeutic Effects." *ACS Pharmacology & Translational Science* 4.2 (April 9, 2021) 563–67. https://doi.org/10.1021/acsptsci.0c00192.

Palamar, Joseph J., et al. "National and Regional Trends in Seizures of Shrooms (Psilocybin) in the United States, 2017–2022." *Drug and Alcohol Dependence* (February 6, 2024) n.p. https://doi.org/10.1016/j.drugalcdep.2024.111086.

Palitsky R., et al. "Importance of Integrating Spiritual, Existential, Religious, and Theological Components in Psychedelic-Assisted Therapies." *JAMA Psychiatry* 80 (2023) 743–49.

Peacock, Caroline, et al. "Spiritual Health Practitioners' Contributions to Psychedelic Assisted Therapy: A Qualitative Analysis." *PLOS ONE* 19.1 (January 2, 2024) 1–23. https://doi.org/10.1371/journal.pone.0296071.

Pew Research Center. "Religious 'Nones' in America: Who They Are and What They Believe." Pew Research Center, January 24, 2024. https://www.pewresearch.org/religion/2024/01/24/religious-nones-in-america-who-they-are-and-what-they-believe/.

Plesa, Patric, and Rotem Petranker. "Psychedelics and Neonihilism: Connectedness in a Meaningless World." *Frontiers in Psychology* 14 (2023) 1–10. https://www.frontiersin.org/articles/10.3389/fpsyg.2023.1125780.

Pollan, Michael. *How to Change Your Mind: What the New Science of Psychedelics Teaches Us about Consciousness, Dying, Addiction, Depression, and Transcendence.* New York: Penguin, 2019.

Presbyterian Church (USA). "Putting Healing Before Punishment." Presbyterian Church (USA), February 14, 2022. https://www.presbyterianmission.org/resource/putting-healing-before-punishment-2018/.

Rahner, Karl. "Do Not Stifle the Spirit!" In vol. 7 of *Theological Investigations*, translated by David Bourke, 72–87. London: Darton, Longman & Todd, 1971.

———. "Experience of the Holy Spirit." In vol. 18 of *Theological Investigations*, translated by Edward Quinn, 189–209. London: Darton, Longman & Todd, 1983.

———. "The Ignatian Mysticism of Joy in the World." In vol. 3 of *Theological Investigations*, translated by Boniface Kruger, 277–93. Baltimore: Helicon, 1967.

———. "Some Implications of the Scholastic Concept of Uncreated Grace." In vol. 1 of *Theological Investigations*, translated by Cornelius Ernst, 297–346. Baltimore: Helicon, 1961.

———. "The Spirituality of the Church of the Future." In vol. 10 of *Theological Investigations*, translated by Peter Hebblethwaite, 143–53. London: Darton, Longman & Todd, 1973.

Raison, Charles L., et al. "Single-Dose Psilocybin Treatment for Major Depressive Disorder: A Randomized Clinical Trial." *JAMA* 330.9 (September 5, 2023) 843–53. https://doi.org/10.1001/jama.2023.14530.

Reardon, Sara. "Psychedelic Treatments Are Speeding towards Approval—but No One Knows How They Work." *Nature* 623 (November 1, 2023) 22–24. https://doi.org/10.1038/d41586-023-03334-6.

Richards, William A. *Sacred Knowledge: Psychedelics and Religious Experiences.* New York: Columbia University Press, 2015.

Rosas, Fernando E., et al. "The Entropic Heart: Tracking the Psychedelic State via Heart Rate Dynamics." *bioRxiv* (November 9, 2023) 1–11. https://doi.org/10.1101/2023.11.07.566008.

Ross, Stephen, et al. "Rapid and Sustained Symptom Reduction Following Psilocybin Treatment for Anxiety and Depression in Patients with Life-Threatening Cancer: A Randomized Controlled Trial." *Journal of Psychopharmacology* 30.12 (December 2016) 1165–80. https://doi.org/10.1177/0269881116675512.

Sanders, James W., and Josjan Zijlmans. "Moving Past Mysticism in Psychedelic Science." *ACS Pharmacology & Translational Science* 4.3 (June 11, 2021) 1253–55. https://doi.org/10.1021/acsptsci.1c00097.

Schimmel, Nina, et al. "Psychedelics for the Treatment of Depression, Anxiety, and Existential Distress in Patients with a Terminal Illness: A Systematic Review." *Psychopharmacology* 239.1 (January 1, 2022) 15–33. https://doi.org/10.1007/s00213-021-06027-y.

Schlag, A. K., et al. "Adverse Effects of Psychedelics: From Anecdotes and Misinformation to Systematic Science." *Journal of Psychopharmacology* 36 (2022) 1–15.

Schner, George P. "The Appeal to Experience." *Theological Studies* 53 (1992) 40–59.

Sells, Michael. "From a History of Mysticism to a Theology of Mysticism." *The Journal of Religion* 73.3 (1993) 390–99.

Simonsson, Otto, et al. "Associations between Lifetime Classic Psychedelic Use and Markers of Physical Health." *Journal of Psychopharmacology* 35.4 (April 1, 2021) 447–52. https://doi.org/10.1177/0269881121996863.

Simonsson, Otto, et al. "Prevalence and Associations of Challenging, Difficult or Distressing Experiences Using Classic Psychedelics." *Journal of Affective Disorders* 326 (April 1, 2023) 105–10. https://doi.org/10.1016/j.jad.2023.01.073.

Sjöstedt-Hughes, Peter. "On the Need for Metaphysics in Psychedelic Therapy and Research." *Frontiers in Psychology* 14 (2023) 1–17. https://www.frontiersin.org/articles/10.3389/fpsyg.2023.1128589.

Smith, Huston. "Do Drugs Have Religious Import?" *The Journal of Philosophy* 61.18 (1964) 517–30. https://doi.org/10.2307/2023494.

———. "Do Drugs Have Religious Import? A Forty Year Follow-Up." In *Higher Wisdom: Eminent Elders Explore the Continuing Impact of Psychedelics*, edited by Roger N. Walsh and Charles S. Grob, 223–39. Albany: State University of New York Press, 2005.

Spiers, Nicholas, et al. "Indigenous Psilocybin Mushroom Practices: An Annotated Bibliography." *Journal of Psychedelic Studies* 1 (February 8, 2024) 2–25. https://doi.org/10.1556/2054.2023.00297.

Stace, W. T. *Mysticism and Philosophy*. New York: St. Martin's, 1960.

Thomas, Owen C. "Theology and Experience." *The Harvard Theological Review* 78 (1985) 179–201.

Timmermann, Christopher, et al. "Psychedelics Alter Metaphysical Beliefs." *Scientific Reports* 11.1 (November 23, 2021) 1–13. https://doi.org/10.1038/s41598-021-01209-2.

United Methodist Church. "Alcohol and Other Drugs." In *The Book of Resolutions of the United Methodist Church*, 156–66. Nashville: United Methodist Publishing, 2016.

Wainwright, William J. "Mysticism." In *The Encyclopedia of Philosophy of Religion*, edited by Stewart Goetz et al., 1–10. Hoboken, NJ: John Wiley & Sons, Ltd, 2021. https://doi.org/10.1002/9781119009924.eopr0255.

Wan, William. "Ecstasy Could Be 'Breakthrough' Therapy for Soldiers, Others Suffering from PTSD." *Washington Post*, April 8, 2023. https://www.washingtonpost.com/national/health-science/ecstasy-could-be-breakthrough-therapy-for-soldiers-others-suffering-from-ptsd/2017/08/26/009314ca-842f-11e7-b359-15a3617c767b_story.html.

Wasson, R. Gordon. "Seeking the Magic Mushroom." *Life* 42.19 (May 13, 1957) 100–20.

Winkelman, Michael James, et al. "The Potential of Psychedelics for the Treatment of Alzheimer's Disease and Related Dementias." *European*

Neuropsychopharmacology 76 (November 1, 2023) 3–16. https://doi. org/10.1016/j.euroneuro.2023.07.003.

Yaden, David B., and Andrew Newberg. *The Varieties of Spiritual Experience: 21st Century Research and Perspectives.* Oxford: Oxford University Press, 2022.

Yaden, David B., et al. "Ethical Issues Regarding Nonsubjective Psychedelics as Standard of Care." *Cambridge Quarterly of Healthcare Ethics* 31.4 (October 2022) 464–71. https://doi.org/10.1017/S0963180122000007X.

Zahl, Simeon. "Affective Augustinianism in the Wild: An Appreciation and a Response." *Journal of Spiritual Formation & Soul Care* 15.1 (May 2022) 164–70.

———. "An Anglican Theology of Grace." *Anglican Theological Review* 104.4 (November 2022) 436–43. https://doi.org/10.1177/00033286221131135.

———. *The Holy Spirit and Christian Experience.* Oxford: Oxford University Press, 2020.

———. "Incongruous Grace as Pattern of Experience." *International Journal of Systematic Theology* 22.1 (January 2020) 60–76. https://doi.org/10. 1111/ijst.12402.

Index

Made in the USA
Las Vegas, NV
23 April 2025

21293334R00100